Social Media Use and Youth Mental Health

Navigating Social Media's Impact on Young People's Mental Health: A Compassionate Guide for Parents and Caregivers

Tina Shelton

More Titles From Tina Shelton

Book 1 - *Gut Health and Fasting for Beginners*

"I Loved the Amazon version so much that I picked up the Audible version as well! Gut Health and Fasting for Beginners (by Tina Shelton) contains a wealth of information for those who are new to the field…Her information is solid and well-presented, you won't get lost in medical jargon. She explains everything. I cannot recommend this book highly enough."

S.R.Settles - *Mentor, Speaker, Coach - Ogden UT, USA*

"Tina Shelton's book, was an amazingly comprehensive text on gut health and fasting. When I first began the book, I assumed it was mainly on fasting, and though it covers fasting in depth it also covers other aspects of gut health, the importance of it, and how to maintain it. Ms. Shelton also did an admirable job of describing the pros and cons of various fasting regimes and the changes the body goes through across hours and even days of fasting. Definitely worth the read."

Charles C. McCormack - *Therapist | Aberdeen, MD Guest faculty Washington School of Psychiatry, USA*

GET YOUR COPY ON AMAZON

GET A 30-DAY FREE TRIAL ON AUDIBLE

Book 2 - *Brain Health and Fasting for Men and Women Aged 40 and Over*

"This book presents, in straightforward language, how fasting can support and enhance brain function as you age. This book offers a balanced perspective, not solely emphasizing the benefits of fasting but also providing detailed information about potential side effects. In my view, it provides a comprehensive yet easily understandable guide for anyone seeking a healthier and more vibrant version of themselves as they age."

Dr. Azar G. Shirazi - *Research Fellow, The University of Manchester - UK*

"Brain Health and Fasting for Men and Women Aged 40 and Over" is a valuable resource for those interested in exploring the potential benefits of fasting for brain health. It offers a holistic approach, combining scientific research with practical guidance to empower readers in their journey toward a vibrant and thriving brain. Whether you're experiencing cognitive issues or simply looking to prevent them, this book promises to be a roadmap to a better mental state."

Tarrent-Arthur Henry - *author and speaker with Maxwell Leadership, and a Disaster Relief and Mental Health Responder*

GET YOUR COPY ON AMAZON

GET A 30-DAY FREE TRIAL ON AUDIBLE SOON

Table of Contents

Introduction:

Navigating the Digital Currents

How many times have you stared at your child and their friends, glued to their phones, wondering what could be so interesting online? How many times has your child been severely upset by something they read or saw online? Perhaps their online encounters have even contributed to or caused mental health conditions, such as depression or anxiety. Your child's online habits may be confusing to you, as we did not grow up in this digital era where we now find ourselves. Many parents feel ill-equipped to deal with the problems they see among their children regarding social media and digital technology.

As a teacher, I am no stranger to the scenarios above. I am a secondary school teacher (pupils of 11–16 years old) in the UK with over 20 years of experience in education and a background in social research and investigative journalism. In recent years I have come to witness anecdotal evidence in the classroom and in schools suggesting that our young people are becoming increasingly dependent on their mobile phones and social media. It is common to see an increasing number of learners tired or sleepy during early lessons and throughout the day. I usually ask the following questions: "What time did you go to sleep?" and "How long did you actually sleep?"

Answers from learners usually vary from two to five hours of sleep, with occasionally a few cases of zero to thirty minutes of sleep. Then the follow-up questions are "What were you doing?" or "Were you doing your homework?" About 50% of the time their answers were convergent: they were spending time on social media platforms such as TikTok, Snapchat, etc. Needless to say lack of sleep affects school performance. From an observational perspective, pupils who are sleep-deprived tend to be grumpy, unfocused, argumentative, uncooperative, display erratic behavior, and have a poor attitude to learning.

Dr. Jean M. Twenge (2017) asked a similar question to her undergraduate students "What do you do with your phone while you sleep? Why?"

Their answers were a profile in obsession. Nearly all her students slept with their phones, putting them under their pillows, on the mattress, or at the very least within arm's reach of the bed. They checked social media websites throughout the night and first thing in the morning.

As I have some positive family experience on the matter after struggling as a parent and as an aunty, coupled with my passion for sharing simple steps to improve the quality of life of people in general, I decided to investigate the matter further. So I invested myself in this book, as an educator, to better understand and empathize with parents and caregivers in need of support. My intention is to provide them with a compassionate guide on how to navigate the impact of social media on their children's mental well-being.

I understand that many other parents and caregivers out there have similar concerns. They are watching their children change before their eyes, and they feel helpless. How can they protect their children against the effects of social media if they don't understand social media in the first place? Well, that's why I have written this book. This book is intended to provide every parent with practical steps on how to establish a relationship with their child and foster positive connections to help prevent mental health conditions due to social media.

Before I go any further, I would like to point out one thing. In this book, you will read the word parent a lot. I know that not every person buying or reading this book is doing so to help their biological child. I believe that the term parent extends to any person who is caring for a child. Whether you are an aunt, grandparent, foster parent, or caretaker, if you are taking care of the physical and emotional needs of a child, you are acting as their parent, and this term applies to you. Families come in many shapes and sizes, and if you are doing this for your "child," I consider you their parent, whether you conceived them or not.

So this book was written to help all of you to navigate the currents of this digital era as parents, and to help your child do the same. There's a lot to cover on this topic, so I hope you are ready to learn. In this book, you will learn the basics of various social media platforms and how they work. You will learn about the most obvious dangers of social media on a child's mental and physical health. You will then learn why you, as a parent, play an integral role in protecting your child from the dangers social media poses to them. We'll discuss how you can help protect your child against these dangers by fostering honest communication, setting boundaries, and promoting digital resilience.

While the use of social media has significant risks, and we do discuss these risks in this book, I also want you to understand that social media can be beneficial for your child if they use it correctly. Therefore, we will consider the advantages of social media and how your child can use social media for creative expression, connecting with like-minded people, and bringing positive change to the world. We'll consider how you can help your child become a responsible digital citizen, and I'll share plenty of real-life examples to show you that the advice shared in this book works.

Make no mistake, however. You will learn as much about yourself and your online habits in this book as you will learn about helping your child. You'll see that much of the advice shared in this book revolves around you setting a good example for your child so they can foster good online habits. This means that you will likely have to change some of your online habits yourself. And while some of the ideas in this book may be met with some resistance, they will significantly improve your child's mental health, their relationship with social media, and your relationship with them.

So, if you are ready to change your child's online habits for the better and improve your communication and relationship with them, you have come to the right place. The nine chapters in this book will challenge and change you, and you will never look at social media or the digital era the same way again. I will be with you every step of the way. You are not alone. I wish you all the best on this informative and transformative journey, and I hope you will finish this book with a much better understanding of the effects of social media on youth mental health and which practical steps you must take to best support your child.

Chapter 1:

The Social Media Landscape—A

Digital Wilderness

You likely already have a good idea of how much social media influences your child. You also use social media daily, so you are no stranger to the effects and importance of social media in our society. In the first chapter of this book, we will discuss the progression of social media, the different social media platforms and their influence over young minds, the statistics of social media use among youth, and the dual nature of social media. An interesting observation was made in an article regarding the targeting of social media on teenagers specifically. The article published in Jehovah's Witness.org, reports the following:

> In the United States, the word "teenager" became popular in the 1940's when marketers began grouping people according to their buying characteristics. Teenagers "were largely in the same place —high school—sharing a common experience, and they were young and open to new things," says the book The Rise and Fall of the American Teenager. "They were, in short, easy to sell to." (*Why Reject the Media*, n.d.)

The article also mentions that nowadays tweens (between 9 and 12) are also targeted since they use social media just as often. This might give you a better idea of why your child is so vulnerable to, and influenced by, social media—for better or worse.

Make no mistake, a lot of good can come from the proper use of social media. Unfortunately, some dangers cannot be avoided. So, let's consider social media in a broader landscape to determine its importance and effect in our current society and for our youth.

Caught in the Stream

According to the *Digital School of Marketing*, "The true strength of social media is influence" (Greyling, 2020). And that is true. While we'll take a deeper dive into the statistics of social media use and the significant influence it has on our youth in another chapter, you must get comfortable with this idea—the aim of social media is to influence people. Whether it's influencing them to buy a product, take out a new type of insurance, try the newest fat-loss miracle, or whatever the case may be, social media is, first and foremost, a marketing tool used to influence your opinions and actions. And this is not a new use for social media. It is the original purpose of social media; it has always been.

Before cell phones and television were standard household items, people would go to the cinemas to watch a movie, or they would buy a newspaper to catch up with the latest news. Before every movie, there were advertisements. Just as there were advertisements on every page in the newspaper. Marketing products, trying to convince you that you have not lived until you have tried the newest Dyson vacuum, that you are a coward if you don't join the war efforts, or that you must purchase the new cookbook that promises to bring your family health and happiness. Though the point of these advertisements was to influence you to buy products or use services, they strongly influenced many parts of the average person's life.

That influence kept growing and progressing, soon becoming the entire aim of advertising and social media. The creation of the idea that you can become as happy/skinny/strong/successful as the person in the advertisement if you do what they do or use the products they use shifted the focus of social media and advertising and essentially put the industry on the trajectory it is today. But two generations ago, social media's reach (and therefore influence) was limited to the people in a town, city, region, or country. It was limited by how far that advertisement could be spread. When home television became more popular, the media's reach widened. However, it was still somewhat limited to specific target audiences.

That quickly changed when smartphones came into the picture. Some of the first social media platforms used included WeChat, Blackberry Messaging (BBM), Snapchat, and Facebook. Instagram and TikTok would later change the face of social media, but more on this later. Soon, everyone had a smartphone and used it to keep up to date with the latest trends. That included social media trends. They would send pictures or memes to their peers. Social media became the primary method of communication. But it also became the primary method of social interaction.

Today, you will often see people sitting next to each other at a café or restaurant. And while they are in each other's presence, they are completely disconnected from one another as both are on their phones. This is true for people from all generations, but it's especially concerning when we see it among today's youth. It has led to children not being able to communicate effectively by using their words. It has also led to the youth allowing their entire identity to be based on their social media presence, how many followers they have, and how in sync they are with the latest trends. This is the danger with social media, which we have predicted for some time now but have not done anything to intercept.

Digital Footprints

Many things have changed since the time we read hard-copy newspapers and went to watch a movie with war propaganda during the commercials. One of those things is how attached we have become to the online world, including social media. Today, there are so many social media applications that you may not know them all. In this section, we will discuss the most popular social media platforms based on their average monthly users and how each platform influences or allures youth—good and bad. These average monthly user statistics are based on the March 2023 statistics in an article of Buffer (Lua, 2023). So, let's consider some of the most popular social media platforms used by tweens (children between 9 and 12) and teens today and what they are used for.

YouTube

YouTube is one of the oldest social media platforms, but is still the most popular. A total of 2.2 billion people use YouTube every month (Lua, 2023). YouTube is used to watch videos on nearly every topic imaginable. Many social media influencers started their journey on YouTube. Whether it's watching funny cat videos or a "day in the life" of their favorite celebrity or influencer, children spend a lot of time on YouTube.

WhatsApp

WhatsApp is the most popular communication platform in the West. With 2 billion monthly users, it's no surprise that you likely don't know anyone who doesn't have WhatsApp or who doesn't use it daily. Tweens, teens, and adults use WhatsApp as their primary form of communication, sending messages, memes, and videos on the platform. WhatsApp also has a call function, allowing you to make phone and video calls on the platform.

Instagram

Instagram is another social media platform most people are familiar with. Like WhatsApp, it also has an average monthly user rate of 2 billion. It is a popular app among people of all ages. This is the platform where social media influencers share the products they use, photos and videos of their daily lives, and their opinions on certain matters. Many of today's youth base their popularity or likeability on their Instagram following. It's not uncommon to see people adopt an entirely different persona on Instagram to make them seem more influential or popular.

WeChat

Before WhatsApp, WeChat was the primary communication app used by all. It is still the most popular app used in Asia, with 1.26 billion monthly users (Lua, 2023). WeChat has many of the same functions as WhatsApp, but it has a few unique ones, including WeChat Pay and more. Like WhatsApp, people also like to share stories of their day through photos and videos on the platform.

TikTok

TikTok has a huge following of 1 billion monthly users, and most of the users on TikTok fall into the 10–19 age group, making it one of the most influential social media platforms for our youth. TikTok is where you can post one-minute videos of absolutely anything you want. Many social media influencers on Instagram and YouTube are also present on TikTok. It is also a popular platform for advertising new products, with the popular phrase "TikTok made me buy it" being spread worldwide.

Sina Weibo

Weibo is the Asian alternative to Twitter. This app is extremely popular across Asia, especially China, with 573 million monthly users. People share their thoughts and opinions on various topics on Weibo through short "microblogs." While Weibo isn't as popular in the West, it is still an influential app, and many messages on Weibo are distributed worldwide through other platforms.

Snapchat

Snapchat is an older app that predates Instagram and many other applications on this list. Still, Snapchat has 557 million active monthly users, making it an influential app today. Like TikTok and Instagram, Snapchat is an app to share your day's videos and photos. It isn't used as a marketing tool quite as often as some other apps, but it is still a way to influence others to try new things.

Twitter

The Weibo of the West, Twitter, also known as X, has 238 million monthly users. While the older generation commonly uses Twitter, many of the youth read Twitter messages. Given how impressionable they are, it comes as no surprise that popular or shocking Twitter messages are often captured and spread across various other social media platforms, broadening its global influence.

Discord

If you are not a gamer, you might have yet to hear of Discord. Discord is an online streaming website that gamers often use to communicate with each other. It has an average monthly user rate of 150 million people. People often connect their headsets or computers with Discord so they can talk to their friends or partners while playing online games.

Twitch

Twitch is like YouTube for gamers and e-sports. Professional and amateur gamers often livestream their gaming tournaments or general gameplay, and users must register and pay a monthly fee to watch their gamer stars play these games. Twitch has 140 million monthly users, making it one of the most popular streaming platforms. Many professional gamers use Twitch as a primary or secondary income.

Mastodon

Mastodon is a brand-new app that gained traction at the end of 2022. It now has a monthly usage of 1.7 million users, growing from 300,000 in just a few months. "Mastodon is a decentralized, open-source software that allows users to set up servers to communicate with each other. Users can create posts of up to 5000 characters and add images, audio, and video" (Lua, 2023).

Numbers and Narratives

Considering how many monthly users use the apps discussed in the previous section, it should be no surprise that many of these users fall into the tween and teen categories. While the average minimum age for using many of the abovementioned social media apps is 18, many children as young as eight also use these apps. Children are younger and younger when they get their first smartphones. While most parents intend the phones to be a safety precaution (so their children can contact them whenever needed), it also leaves the door open for using these social media apps.

According to the U.S. Surgeon General, "Up to 95% of youth ages 13–17 report using a social media platform, with more than a third saying they use social media "almost constantly"" (*Social Media and Youth*, 2023). This is not a surprising statistic and is in line with what we see in schools and at home. According to the Surgeon General, the most popular apps this age group uses are Twitter, Instagram, and TikTok. While there are some advantages to using social media, there are also many downsides. One of them is that there is a strong connection between social media use and mental health conditions among teenagers.

Social media use has been connected to various mental and physical health problems, including depression, anxiety, suicidal thoughts, self-harm, and sleep problems. Dr. Gary Small, a professor of psychiatry, "discovered that kids' time on powerful electronic devices was actually changing their brains" (Kersting, 2020). I have witnessed the effect of sleep problems on mental health in my own classroom. Teenagers who spend hours on social media at night get less sleep and poor quality sleep. This leads to them being exhausted at school, which affects their academic performance. It also affects their mood. When people don't get enough sleep, they become irritable, making it more difficult to work with them and entice them to cooperate during class activities. Poor academic performance also contributes to mental health conditions, including anxiety and depression. As such, social media contributes to these conditions in more ways than one.

"Furthermore, some researchers believe that social media exposure can overstimulate the reward center in the brain and, when the stimulation becomes excessive, can trigger pathways comparable to addiction" (*Social Media and Youth*, 2023). This is even more concerning. I recently read a study on dopamine detoxing, where you detox your brain's reward system to enable it to find certain actions rewarding again. Social media is a plague on the brain's dopamine system, as it is so easy to find relief or a quick distraction with social media. This desensitizes your brain to actual rewards, making it more difficult to feel enticed to do certain activities. Even natural dopamine-releasing activities, such as exercise, are no longer as rewarding to the brain.

Social Media: The Good, the Bad, and the Ugly

While it's easy to read this first chapter and think that no good can come from social media and that we should simply forbid our children from using it, social media is not just bad. Many advantages of social media cannot be ignored. Furthermore, prohibiting teenagers from using social media will only create a divide between you. They will find ways of using social media. They will do so behind your back and won't feel comfortable telling you if something negative or dangerous has happened on social media. Therefore, learning how to navigate social media rather than prohibit it is important. Let's consider some of social media's pros, cons, and dangers for today's youth.

Advantages of Social Media

Social media has many advantages, making it impossible to classify it as being solely negative. Some positive aspects of social media are:

- It gives you a sense of creative expression. Social media is a great platform to express your creativity and get new ideas. Whether it's sharing your artwork, music, fashion sense, or photography, there are social media platforms for nearly every art form.

- It allows you to stay connected with friends and family. Social media allows you to keep in touch with friends and family no matter where they are. You can talk to them, share inspirational or funny messages, or simply connect with them via chat.

- It exposes you to new people and experiences. Social media platforms, like Instagram, allow you to connect with people worldwide. You can learn many new things, including new skills and places to visit. You can also learn about different cultures and increase your cultural awareness.

- It allows you to connect with like-minded people. If you have a specific interest that your friends don't share, you may find like-minded people online with whom you can connect and share your experiences. This can also help people with disabilities or certain challenges feel less isolated from the world, and they can connect with people who share their challenges.

Disadvantages of Social Media

Unfortunately, despite social media's many advantages, some downsides are impossible to ignore. These disadvantages may affect people of all ages. However, since teenagers are impressionable and more sensitive than adults, they are especially susceptible to these risks. The disadvantages of social media include the following:

It Can Isolate You

While social media can help you connect with loved ones, it can also cause you to feel isolated from them. If your child had a falling out with their friends or sees their friends doing fun things without them, it could make them feel isolated or alone.

It Causes Disconnection

We've discussed the scenario where teenagers sit beside each other but are preoccupied with their phones. This also happens in the home. I've spent hours trying to connect with my children while they are too busy on their phones even to notice I am talking to them. This is a common problem with social media, as it disconnects you from the present moment.

It Leads to Self-Loathing

Many teenagers (and adults) compare themselves to others on social media. They watch what others are doing and feel inferior because they don't have enough money, skills, or the opportunity to do the same things. This can lead to self-loathing or feeling inferior to others.

It Can Cause Personality Changes

Since teenagers are so impressionable, they might start changing their behavior to "fit in" with the influencers they see on social media. Your child may feel like their current behavior isolates them from others, and they might change it. While some behavioral changes are normal as your child grows up, others are deliberate and unwanted.

Dangers of Social Media

Social media can lead to dangerous situations where your child's well-being or life may be threatened. The dangers of social media include the following:

- Social media is linked to mental health problems. Depression, self-harm, and suicide are mental health conditions connected to social media. These are serious conditions that may lead to physical harm or even death.

- Social media may encourage children to engage in dangerous behavior. If certain people influence your child, they might engage in dangerous behavior to try and be like that person or fit in. This can be as simple as piercing their body to something as reckless as cliff jumping. A few years ago, a challenge was going around called The Blue Whale Challenge, which challenged teenagers to complete 50 tasks over 50 days. The final task: taking your own life. Teenagers are susceptible to apps and challenges like these, which may lead to unnecessary deaths and heartache.

- Social media is a prowling ground for perverts and groomers. While many people on social media have good intentions, there are also those with ill intentions. Some predators, child abusers, and abductors scour social media and groom vulnerable children. In some cases, they convince the child to meet them somewhere, allowing them to abduct or abuse the child.

- Social media exposes children to inappropriate content. Whether it's sending or receiving, social media provides the means for gaining access to inappropriate content. Children are exposed to pornographic images, abusive or degrading language use, racial slurs, and content containing explicit violence or abuse. Despite your best efforts to protect your children against these factors, they are just a click away on social media.

- Social media creates an unrealistic sense of body image and self-worth. The more children are on social media, the more they will compare themselves to others they see on it. This might lead them to develop a negative body image. Their self-worth might also be affected as they think they are worth less than the successful people they see on social media. Furthermore, since social media provides the grounds for body shaming and online bullying, these factors may become an even bigger problem for your child.

- Social media leads to an obsession with likes or comments. Children may start connecting online likes and comments with popularity and self-worth. This might lead them to obsess over how many people like their content. It might also lead to engaging in dangerous behavior for the sake of likes and comments. Furthermore, negative comments may severely affect their mood, mental health, and self-confidence.

Key Takeaway From Chapter One

There are many social media platforms on which teenagers spend their time, including YouTube, Instagram, TikTok, WhatsApp, and more. Social media has become more influential and popular as smartphone technology has improved. Unfortunately, while social media has some advantages, such as giving your child an artistic outlet or allowing them to connect with their friends, there are also several disadvantages. Social media is linked to various mental health conditions and exposes children to negative factors, such as suicide and predators.

Chapter 2:

Understanding Youth Mental

Health and Social Media Use

Now that you have a better understanding of the different types of social media and how they influence teenagers, we should consider the effects of these social media platforms on youth mental health. By understanding how social media is connected to mental health conditions, you can gain a deeper understanding of how social media is affecting your child and learn to identify and manage these risks.

As mentioned in the previous chapter, you may think that if you prohibit your child from using social media, they will not be at risk for these mental health conditions. But that is simply not the case. Abstinence is not the solution here. First, we must recognize the problem; then, we can work together to find a solution. So, let's consider the effects of social media on the mental health of the youth.

Behind the Screen

You may think your child is not at risk for mental health conditions because they live happy, healthy lives. But even if that is true, you will find that this doesn't eliminate the risk of mental health conditions. As your child grows up, they will be exposed to more situations that might trigger a mental health condition. Tweens and teenagers are sensitive to criticism and stress—they don't always know how to manage these emotions and the situations that cause them. "Teens tend to express their depression in ways different from those of adults, so be alert to major changes in your child's behavior, eating habits, moods, sleep patterns, or social interactions—especially if the changes persist for weeks" (*Teen Depression—Why*, n.d.). As such, they are at greater risk for internalizing these feelings, increasing their chances of developing a mental health condition.

Understanding mental health conditions and how they present in tweens and teens can help you recognize the symptoms and get your child the help they need. Unfortunately, social media plays a significant role in youth mental health. According to the *World Health Organization (WHO)*, 14% of children aged 10–19 struggle with at least one mental health condition (*Mental Health of Adolescents*, 2021). The sad part is that many of these cases go undiagnosed—either because the child doesn't admit to needing help or because the parents don't realize their child needs it.

The WHO also indicates that depression, anxiety, and behavioral disorders are among the most common mental health conditions our youth face. In addition, teenagers may suffer from additional challenges, including low self-esteem, self-doubt, and self-worth problems. Some of these problems arise due to social media, while all of these conditions can be increased by social media—knowingly or subconsciously.

Anxiety Amongst Children

Anxiety is one of the biggest mental health problems teenagers face. Dr. Kersting (2020) explains "Anxiety is now the number-one type of disability we deal with. At my private counseling practice, I now receive more referrals for middle school children with major anxiety disorders over a one-year period than I used to receive in a ten-year period." This condition is more common amongst older teenagers (aged 15–19) but can arise at any age. Teenagers often experience anxiety because they feel a lot of pressure in various aspects of their lives, including:

- **Pressure to perform:** Children often feel pressured to do well in school, have a social life with many friends, and participate in various extracurricular activities. This pressure may trigger anxiety disorder if not managed.

- **Puberty:** Puberty brings about many changes in a child's life, including physical and emotional changes. They might experience more intense feelings, even if they don't understand why. They might also feel isolated from their friends, especially if they experience puberty earlier or later than their peers. This could lead to anxiety.

- **The desire to fit in:** No matter how individual or strong-willed, children want to fit in and be accepted by their peers. If they don't make friends easily or aren't accepted, they might feel isolated or experience low self-esteem—leaving a gap for anxiety to fester.

Children deal with a lot more pressure than we realize, and if they aren't taught how to manage this pressure or offered the right kind of support during stressful times, they might internalize this pressure, leading to anxiety disorder. There are various kinds of anxiety disorders. In general, the symptoms of this disorder include the following:

- Difficulty concentrating

- Increased irritability

- Withdrawal from friends or social activities

- Self-consciousness

- Sensitivity to criticism (even when meant as a joke)

- Trouble sleeping

- Poor grades at school

- Unwillingness to participate in after-school activities

- Emotional outbursts

- Recurring fears and worries about past or future events

- Constantly seeking approval or reassurance

- Chronic illnesses, such as headaches, stomach aches, nausea

- Avoiding new or challenging situations

- Substance abuse

Anxiety can be difficult to spot in children, especially since they are often exposed to stressful situations, such as exams, school tasks, and sporting events. If your child starts showing the above-mentioned symptoms and they just don't seem themselves, it might indicate they are struggling with anxiety.

Depression Amongst Children

Depression is almost as prevalent among children and teenagers as anxiety. It's an extremely concerning condition, especially when children younger than 12 present with symptoms. Depression doesn't always have a clear cause, like other mental health conditions. Unfortunately, depression can have detrimental effects on a child's well-being. It can lead to isolation, self-harm, low self-esteem, or suicide.

The problem with depression is that it isn't always easy to spot, especially among tweens and teenagers, as they typically undergo many behavioral changes. Therefore, depression may go undetected for some time, increasing the effects this condition has on your child's mental and physical well-being. Symptoms of depression may look different for every child, but the most common symptoms to look out for include the following:

- Crying for no apparent reason or constant sadness

- Emotional bluntness or not expressing any emotions

- Lack of personal hygiene

- Emotional outbursts

- Self-isolation

- Constant negativity and negative self-talk

- Loss of interest in activities they usually enjoy

- Refusal to bond with family members

- Not getting along with family or friends

- Increased self-criticism

- Concentration problems

- Poor performance

- Changes in appetite

- Sleeping often and constant fatigue

- Substance abuse

- Self-harm

- Suicidal thoughts or expressions. For example, if a child starts saying things like, "I wish I were never born," or "You would be better off without me."

These are signs that something might be off with your child's mental health. If you notice any of these symptoms or get the sense that your child is not doing well emotionally, you should talk with them to check on their emotional well-being or suggest they see a therapist if they don't want to talk with you. In either case, determining the cause of their depression is crucial for their improved well-being.

Low Self-Esteem Amongst Children

Both depression and anxiety may lead to low self-esteem among children. But other factors also affect a child's self-esteem. As mentioned before, and as you likely already know, children are extremely sensitive and impressionable. This means that even the slightest changes in their schedule or circumstances can lead to lower self-esteem. Since children undergo so many changes in their lives, both at school and on a personal level, it is no surprise that their self-esteem may dip occasionally. Here are some examples of factors that may lead to a child's low self-esteem:

- **Puberty:** Puberty brings many emotional and physical changes in a child's life. If they experience puberty earlier or later than their peers, they might feel isolated, leading to lower self-esteem. Furthermore, as their bodies change, they will feel more self-conscious, which might also affect their self-esteem.

- **Changing to a new school or grade:** If your child used to achieve good grades without putting in too much effort, they might experience a sudden drop in their grades when starting a new, more difficult school year. Furthermore, if they move to a new school, they might also experience additional challenges, which could lead to lower self-esteem.

- **Diverging interests:** As children grow up, their interests start changing. This is a great thing, but it could lead to feeling insecure, especially if their interests diverge from those of their friends. In this case, they might start feeling isolated or "strange," which could negatively affect their self-esteem.

- **Losing friends:** As a child's interests start changing, they naturally drift apart from some friends. But they might start feeling isolated or alone if they don't make new friends who share their interests. They might also get excluded from parties and events, which harms their self-esteem.

- **Bullies:** Bullies are a normal occurrence in schools. As hard as we try, we cannot always protect our children from bullies. If your child experiences bullying at school, they might develop lower self-esteem, especially if they are bullied frequently or the bully attacks their self-worth.

Children and Self-Doubt

When your children are small, they radiate self-confidence. They feel unstoppable like they can do anything they set their minds to. Unfortunately, that feeling rarely lasts forever. The older children get, the more challenges they encounter. And while failing is a natural part of life, it can lead to children doubting themselves. They might doubt whether they can accomplish something or if they are good enough to make the school team, make friends with someone, or get college acceptance. These feelings can lead to self-doubt, a condition in which your child doubts their abilities.

Self-doubt is a normal part of life, but it can become problematic when it prevents your child from doing things they enjoy or pursuing their goals. Self-doubt can also affect your child's self-confidence, which can affect their self-esteem. This is why it is crucial to encourage and motivate your child not to give up when they fail at something. Helping them see things differently can make them feel more motivated and might combat self-doubt. It's also important to pay attention to your child's self-talk, as this will give you an indication of their self-esteem.

For example, if your child has been talking negatively about themselves, saying they will never be accepted into a college, chosen for a team, or pass a certain class, it indicates that they are dealing with feelings of self-doubt. Unaddressed self-doubt can lead to depression or anxiety, so it is crucial to address self-doubt and boost your child's confidence as soon as possible. Even children who seem extremely confident struggle with these feelings sometimes.

Children and Compromised Self-Worth

Self-doubt, lower self-esteem, depression, and anxiety may lead to a child developing a compromised self-worth. They might feel like they are not worthy of love, attention, or anything good in life. This can also cause depression or anxiety, especially if they constantly need to prove themselves to others. Unfortunately, many of the factors that lead to lower self-esteem also influence a child's self-worth. Failure, bullying, and self-isolation might lead a child to think that they are no longer worthy of good things. If your child cannot overcome their compromised self-worth, it may lead to depression, self-harm, or suicidal thoughts.

A compromised self-worth can also affect various other aspects of your child's life. For example, if they have a lowered self-worth, they might think they deserve to be treated poorly by others. This can affect their friendships and relationships later. They might feel that someone is justified for bullying them or not treating them with the respect they truly deserve. Having a compromised self-worth can also lead to being afraid to live up to their potential, which can hold your child back and prevent them from chasing their dreams. Compromised self-worth can harm a child's self-image.

These thoughts may stem from having low self-esteem or a bad self-image. For example, if your child thinks they are ugly, stupid, or unlikeable, they might start doubting their self-worth, giving way to more negative feelings. The following signs can indicate that your child may be suffering from low self-worth:

- Feeling like they deserve to be treated poorly.

- Not wanting to participate in group activities for fear of letting their friends/family down.

- Not wanting to try and make new friends because they feel like they don't deserve them.

- Attracting negative thoughts or taking criticism very seriously.

- Not feeling deserving of praise or recognition.

- Always feeling like they could have done better.

- Constantly apologizing for small mistakes or things they consider to be mistakes.

- Difficulty accepting love or affection from others. They might not open up fully to a new person, as they are always waiting for the other shoe to drop or for that person to realize that they have made a mistake and move on. They don't connect well with others as they feel this will protect them from getting hurt.

Before we discuss the link between these mental health conditions and social media, I would like to clarify one thing: It is not your fault as a parent or guardian if your child suffers from one of these conditions. As parents, we try our best to support our children and raise them to be positive and healthy. Unfortunately, despite our best efforts, that's not always the case. These mental health conditions are worrisome for many parents. And while there are probably better ways of handling certain situations than you may have in the past, it does not mean that your child's mental health condition is your fault. You will learn how to help your child navigate their condition in this book, but you should never feel like you are the cause. That said, let's consider one of the true culprits in youth mental health—social media.

The Linkage

There is a strong correlation between social media and youth mental health. This is not only true for children and teenagers, but also for college students and adults. The problem with social media is that even though it provides a space for communication, creative expression, and connecting with like-minded people, it also provides a space for an entirely new form of bullying, social isolation, and lowered self-esteem.

As Bailey Parnell explained in a Ted Talk (2017), a few problems come to light when using social media. One of these problems is known as the highlight reel.

Social Media and the Highlight Reel

The highlight reel, as explained by Parnell (2017), is a phenomenon that arises when we compare our daily lives with what other people post on social media. When you post pictures on social media, you post the pictures where you look your best. Your hair looks nice, your skin is glowing, you are dressed fashionably, and you are doing something newsworthy—which is why you are sharing it in the first place. The problem is that other people see the images that you post and falsely compare their daily lives with these photos.

They think to themselves, "Why isn't my life that glamorous?" or "Why don't I get to travel and see the world? She's doing it, and she's my age!" Although the pictures posted on social media do not paint a full picture of someone's life, we start comparing our lives with other people's highlight reels. We consider ourselves inferior to others because we don't lead the same glamorous lives they do, even if those parts of their lives are merely a few photos from a short holiday and not the whole story. Just like us, children do the same thing.

They compare their everyday lives with what they see on social media. Suppose they see celebrities, influencers, or popular kids at school dressing a certain way, hanging out at specific places, or engaging in certain behaviors. They start comparing themselves with these people—even if what those people post on social media is not a true representation of their real lives. They become obsessed with the highlight reel and feel inferior to others based on this false notion. As you can imagine, that can certainly lead to several mental health conditions, including anxiety (fear of not fitting in), depression, and lowered self-esteem or self-worth. And that is not the only threat social media poses.

Social Media and FOMO

FOMO, or fear of missing out, is a common acronym used by children worldwide. Social media certainly increases FOMO by giving your child a clear picture of what they might miss out on. This also leads to a "compare and despair" culture, where children compare their lives with what they see on social media and feel like they are missing out. Like the highlight reel, children watch what others do on social media. They see where others are spending their time, what they are buying, and how they are dressing, and they feel that they need to do the same if they wish to fit in.

Social media also serves as another space for bullying. For example, if your child had a falling out with their friends, the friends might post photos or videos of them doing something fun without your child, making them feel isolated or rejected. As you can imagine, this can increase the risk of several mental health conditions, including depression and social anxiety. While it is natural to feel like you are missing out when you see others doing something you cannot do, it becomes a problem when your FOMO is linked to unrealistic expectations.

Children might not always understand that what they see on social media and what they compare themselves to is an unrealistic representation of someone else's life. They might also not always understand or accept that not everyone has the same privileges. For example, if your child sees others on social media wearing a certain brand of clothes, eating at certain restaurants, or frequenting a specific spot, they might think they will fit in if they do the same. The reality though is that not everyone can afford the lifestyle being promoted on social media, and it might create a feeling of being isolated or missing out.

The Link Between Social Media and Youth Mental Health

The two problems discussed above are by no means the only risks social media poses. These are merely some of your child's challenges when using social media platforms. There are various others to consider, including pressure to fit in, dangers associated with social media platforms (grooming and peer pressure), dangerous challenges like the Blue Whale Challenge discussed in Chapter 1, pornography, cyberbullying, and more. The fact is that social media may harm your child's mental health in various ways. It can significantly contribute to various mental health conditions, including anxiety and depression.

Social media may exacerbate these problems by exposing your child to more factors. Bullying that occurs at school may follow them home. A simple mistake they make might become something that they can never outlive. And because children are so sensitive to emotional triggers, something that wouldn't necessarily bother an adult can stir various emotions in a child and become something they can never escape. Furthermore, social media may also be the cause of mental health conditions. Since children are vulnerable and exposed to social media, a child can fall prey to mental health problems, no matter how emotionally strong he/she is in real life.

One of the big problems of social media is that it is impossible to monitor what children are exposed to. They might be watching TikTok videos of makeup tutorials when the next moment, a pornographic video pops up on their stream. They might be watching fitness content and are then exposed to body shaming or advertisements trying to sell them the latest weight loss miracle, making them feel like they need it. Social media can expose a child to many factors that may harm their self-esteem, giving rise to mental health conditions.

Stories in the Shadows

There are countless examples on the internet of how social media has led to or exacerbated mental health conditions among youth. Reading these stories is extremely worrying, as it gives you a clear image of just how serious the problem really is. But reading internet stories can only do so much. It's when the problems hit home that you really become aware of the issues. As a teacher, I've had countless experiences with the effects of social media on youth mental health.

Just recently, I had a mother coming to me for advice, desperate to help her child who had been struggling with pornography. Since the internet is filled with sites where you can watch pornography for free, and without giving your real age, it is a challenging problem to address. And this mother was not the only one experiencing these struggles. As a parent, it is heartbreaking to see your child suffer or be exposed to factors you have tried your best to protect them from. It can be frustrating not knowing how to help them.

I've witnessed children being bullied by their peers on social media. One semester they are bright and bubbly, excelling at school and making friends wherever they go. The next semester, they are targeted by bullies at school and home through social media. They become withdrawn and emotionally blunt, and their academic performance suffers as a result. This leaves the door open for mental health conditions to take root. These children are susceptible to depression and anxiety, which have the potential to ruin their lives.

One article shared on *ABC News* (Hamilton-Smith, 2018) tells the story of two best friends who shared their experiences on social media. The two girls, Gabby and Jennifer, had been best friends since age six. Their need to be perfect on social media led to self-loathing, eating disorders, and self-harm. Both girls struggled with their image and would play a game where they listed as many things as they could think of that they hated about themselves. They became anxious and depressed and started self-harming as a way to give an outlet to their feelings. The article also states that these girls know of very few people who have not experienced similar feelings.

Singer-songwriter Billie Eilish explains how social media (specifically online porn) affected her mental health as a child. Eilish says that she was exposed to pornography at the age of 11, and that it really "messed with her brain." It affected her relationships later in life, as she did not say no to activities that were not good or acceptable because she had been exposed to these things when watching porn (Reuters, 2021). Furthermore, she said that she suffered from nightmares for a long time as many of the pornographic images she was exposed to contained violent scenes (especially towards women).

Unfortunately, these stories are merely the tip of the iceberg about the effects of social media on youth mental health. The chances are good that your child or their friends have had similar experiences. Considering how difficult a child's life is today and how many factors are working against your child's happiness and well-being, it is up to us, parents and guardians, to protect them as much as possible and to prevent them from experiencing emotional distress and mental health conditions so many others have had to endure because of social media.

Key Takeaway From Chapter 2

While children are generally resilient and confident when they are young, this changes as they get older. Puberty is a big reason for the behavioral changes in your child. They become more self-conscious, and their self-esteem may decrease because of the emotional and physical changes they experience. Anxiety and depression are two of the most common mental health conditions among children, and children as young as 12 have experienced these conditions. Children also experience low self-esteem, self-doubt, and compromised self-worth.

Unfortunately, these factors are often linked with social media. The need for perfection on social media, combined with a fear of missing out, comparing themselves with the highlight reel of others, and being bullied online, can lead to mental health conditions or exacerbate existing conditions. There are countless examples online of how social media contributes to mental health conditions among youth.

Giving your child unrestricted access to social media is like putting them on a horse without proper training.
A recipe for disaster.

Chapter 3:

Becoming a Digital Sherpa—A

Parent's Role

Considering the damaging effects social media may have on your child, especially regarding their mental health and overall well-being, it is no surprise that parents and guardians all over the world are desperately searching for ways to improve communication with their children and discover how they can protect their children from the effects of social media. I have felt that way as a parent and aunt, and as a teacher, I have dealt with many distressed parents before.

Fortunately, this chapter will guide you in doing just that. If you want to protect your children from social media without robbing them of its advantages, you must learn to meet them halfway. That means learning about social media yourself and understanding the pros and cons. Only then will you be able to communicate with your child in a way they understand and clearly explain the safety precautions when using social media without making them feel they need to hide something from you. So, let's consider how you can bridge the gap between generations and protect your children against the dangers of social media.

Parenting in Pixels: Bridging the Gap Between Generations

As parents, we often feel disconnected from our children as they grow up. They go from needing us for everything (from a scraped knee to opening a juice box) to being embarrassed to be seen with us. And while it is a natural—though heartbreaking—part of them growing up, it can also cause a lot of miscommunication and secretive behavior. The *U.S. Surgeon General's Advisory* booklet of 2023 notes that "Parents face significant challenges in managing children and adolescents' use of social media applications, and youth are using social media at increasingly earlier ages" (*Social Media and Youth*, 2023).

This means your children may start disconnecting from you at a much younger age than expected as they become more attached to social media. If your child doesn't feel like they can come to you with their problems without being judged for it, they simply won't. They will do things behind your back, keep secrets, and if they get in trouble, they won't feel comfortable coming to you for help.

No parent wants that to happen; it is heart-wrenching when you one day wake up and realize that you don't have as close a relationship with your child as you would have liked. But that doesn't have to be the case. You can improve your relationship with your child and help them feel confident when talking to you by learning to speak their language—or walking in their shoes. And as you already know from observing your child, a lot of their time and focus is on social media. This is where they communicate with friends, express their creativity, and keep updated with fashion trends, music, and more.

So, if you want to position yourself in a way that makes it easier for your child to come to you with their problems or even just to feel a closer bond with them by observing their interests and passions, learning to navigate the world of social media will definitely count in your favor. However, doing so is much easier said than done, and getting your child to accept you into this part of their life might also prove challenging.

How can you cross the digital divide and connect with your child through a shared interest on social media? Let's consider it in closer detail.

Crossing the Digital Divide: Addressing the Challenges of Parenting in the Tech Era

We all want our children to be safe—it is one of the primary goals of every parent. But since the rise of social media, children have started facing challenges that parents are unaware of. You might have grown up without a cell phone or even a television, much less 24/7 access to social media. This creates a generational gap between you and your child where you don't speak the same language. For example, you might have grown up playing outside, building forts, camping in the wilderness, and exploring outside over the weekends. These activities are familiar to you, and you can easily explain the dangers of snakes, strangers, and poisonous berries to your child.

But your child grows up playing video games, streaming YouTube videos, and following fanatics on social media. This is unexplored terrain for you, and you may have no idea how to warn your child about the dangers of social media, let alone teach them how to use it safely. As a result, any effort you make to connect with your child on this front and any safety advice you may try to give them may come off as "preaching." As you may remember from your experiences as a teenager, having a preachy or overbearing parent is no fun and will only foster resentment and disconnect.

Therefore, you must follow the right steps when bridging the gap between generations, especially if you face challenges when navigating technology. Here are some steps to keep an open relationship with your children as they embrace life on social media.

Be Firm But Respectful

Parents tend to be either too lax or too strict regarding their children and social media use. They either give their children all the space in the world or insist on having full control over their children's lives. Neither extreme is the best option. Instead, you should try to find a middle ground. One where your child understands that there are certain rules when using social media (such as which websites they are allowed to access, how much time they might spend on social media, and what information they are allowed to share), but also that they feel free to express themselves on the platforms and use social media to enrich their lives.

Some parents reason that they have complete access to their child's phone because they pay for it. While that is true to some extent, invading your child's privacy by reading their messages to their friends is like reading your child's journal—it should not be done. Therefore, you should find a balance between monitoring your child's social media use (ensuring they are safe) and giving them the privacy every child and teenager wants and needs.

Familiarize Yourself With the Different Social Media Platforms

It is extremely difficult to tell someone what they can and cannot do if you don't understand how something functions. Imagine trying to coach a sporting team in a sport you don't know the first thing about.

For example, a mother approached me and complained that her son, 15, was spending far too much time playing video games with friends in the neighborhood and that his general behavior had worsened. I suggested she play with him. Although reluctant at first, she understood it was the way to understand him and control what activities he could do online— she started doing so with some success. By that, I mean her relationship/communication with her son improved!

The same is true when trying to set up boundaries on social media if you don't know or understand the platform. You don't necessarily have to be on a platform yourself. However, learning the basics, like what the platform is used for (as discussed in Chapter 1), will give you a better idea of the advantages and potential risks of that platform.

Understanding the difference between Twitch and Twitter can help you guide your child in setting suitable boundaries for each platform. You will gain a deeper understanding of their interests, and you can learn more about the platform and its potential uses yourself. This makes it easier to guide your children when using the platform, and you can properly explain the risks of it to them, even if you don't wish to use the platform yourself.

Don't Intrude on Your Child's Privacy

As mentioned before, intruding on your child's privacy is not the way to go about protecting them against the risks of social media. If your child finds out that you have been reading their messages or tracking their social media use without their knowledge, they will feel betrayed and hurt. This is one of the easiest ways to lose your connection with your child. Therefore, while it is fine to have some way of monitoring your child's social media use and ensuring they are safe and responsible, doing so behind their back is not the best approach.

Instead, you can request an open-door policy (more on this in the following section) with your child and their devices. This allows you to monitor their social media and online use without them feeling like you are not respecting their privacy. Of course, how strict you are with your child's privacy depends on their age. Younger children can be watched more closely as they are less knowledgeable of the risks of social media. Teaching them about the risks at a younger age is also important.

Set Clear Boundaries and Enforce Them

On the opposite end of the spectrum is the issue of boundaries. Boundaries are important in all areas of life, including social media. Setting clear boundaries for your child and social media will help keep them safe and let them know that you understand they want their freedom, but they have to understand the risks and responsibilities that come with it. Of course, to do so, you must also understand how social media platforms work and which risks they might pose. A good boundary to enforce, for example, is to restrict your child from sharing personal information (such as their address, cell phone number, or which school they attend) on social media.

Another important boundary is to prohibit your child from meeting with people they have met online in person alone. If your child has done so before, it's important to discuss the potential dangers of doing so with them and clarify that this behavior is unacceptable. Enforcing the idea that social media is a privilege, not a right, will make it clear to your child that you can remove their access to social media if necessary. While it might sound harsh, it is a necessary step in ensuring their safety and raising children who understand the risks that come with social media and online presence.

If worst comes to worst, we, as parents, can also enforce certain boundaries regarding social media use. While our children might not be ecstatic about it, it will ultimately help them better understand how to use social media correctly. Smartphone devices come with built-in apps already installed, like Mail, Google, and Facetime. You can choose which apps and features appear on your child's device. You can also alter the features in the Game Centre to enhance your child's safety and privacy when playing games and block App Store purchases if you wish to prevent them from making purchases without your consent.

Listen When Your Child Shares Something With You

It is easy to say you want to share in your child's interests. But oftentimes, when children show or tell us about something they have seen on social media, we stop listening as we feel (subconsciously) that what they are talking about doesn't matter. While their information might not always be the most interesting, listening intently will help them feel appreciated and can make you feel more connected and involved with their lives. Since younger children are more inclined to share their interests with their parents, you must pay attention when they do so at a younger age.

This will make them more open to sharing with you when they grow up, and they won't feel as inclined to hide things from you. Furthermore, you'll get to see what they are interested in, which can help you bond with them as they get older. Listening to your child's stories and watching them share information with you can also help you monitor their activities. This makes it easier to detect if something unsavory is happening with your child on social media. It also allows you to guide them better when they are in danger or when they partake in risky behavior online.

Setting Up a Family Contract

When you have older children, it might be worthwhile to set up a family contract explaining all the house rules and consequences for breaking them. This contract should not be aimed at shaming or punishing your child but should instead help them understand the consequences of their actions and why you don't want them participating in certain behaviors online, such as watching pornography or engaging in risky online behavior. This contract can help your child determine why these behaviors are dangerous and how they should react when exposed to these situations (talk with you about it, turn their computer off, report the problem, and more).

The exact details of the contract will differ from family to family based on what you consider harmful behavior. You can also review the contract every few months and add more information to it as your child ages or you realize they are exposed to more dangers. Having a written form of actionable steps will help your child identify risky online behavior and give them a deeper understanding of why this behavior is risky, to begin with.

Fostering Mutual Learning Between Parents and Youth

Of course, just because you should take the step to bridge the gap and show an interest in your child's social media and online presence, it does not mean it will be easy. Our children grew up with technology that we never even dreamed of as children. This makes it difficult for parents to connect with their children in this regard, especially if they don't know what social media is about or how to use or understand the platforms their children are using. Therefore, if you want to learn to interact with your child about social media and teach them to use it safely, you must be open to learning from them.

Fostering mutual learning and communication between yourself and your child will not only bridge the generational gap between you but will also assure your child that you are open to communicating with them and supporting them in everything they do. Unfortunately, children might not want you to be on social media, especially when they get older. It is, therefore, important that you manage this time with them correctly to prevent them from retaliating or shutting you out.

Ideally, the younger your child, the easier it will be to connect with them on this front. Younger children are more open to sharing their experiences with their parents and might have more patience when helping you set up your social media accounts and more. So, if you want to foster mutual learning between parents and youth, it's important to follow the right steps when approaching your child. You may be the parent, but they likely have more experience in the realm of social media. Here are some steps you can take to foster open communication with your child and keep them safe on social media.

Step 1: Find Out Which Social Media Platform Your Child is Using

The first step to learning to connect with your child over social media is to discover which social media platforms they use. You can do this by asking them what they are keeping busy with and asking some general questions about the platform. For example, you can ask them what the platform is used for, what they enjoy about it, and what interesting information/content they enjoy seeing on it. Your tone and approach are important now, as you don't want your child to feel like you are lecturing them or checking up on them. Instead, use a friendly and inquisitive tone and genuinely show interest when they talk to you about the platform and how it works.

Step 2: Consider How You Can Connect With Your Child on Social Media

After you have opened discussions about the platform, you can create your account and start exploring the platform. You don't have to install all the same social media platforms as your child. Instead, choose one you think you will connect with best and learn to use this platform. Watching YouTube videos or tutorials will give you a great idea of how you can use the platform. Furthermore, you can consider how you can connect with your child on the platform. For example, if you are interested in watching Marvel movies, you can follow accounts related to this topic and share any interesting or funny information you find with your child (either on the platform or in real life).

Step 3: Which Learning Opportunities Are There on This Platform?

When learning to navigate the platform, you can also consider if there are any learning opportunities on the platform for your child. For example, are there any educational platforms where they can enhance a skill? Are there any areas of this social media platform that could be beneficial/dangerous for your child? Exploring the platform yourself will give you a better idea of the pros and cons of the platform and the risks you may have to warn your child about. Furthermore, you can consider if there are any other opportunities on this platform. Perhaps you can help your child start their first side income or business using the platform.

Step 4: Consider How You Can Ask Your Child for Help

If you get stuck at a certain point when using the platform, you can ask your child for help. In this case, you must approach the situation correctly. Failing to do so may lead to an argument. Since children are prone to mood changes (and generally aren't the most patient), you may have to practice some restraint when asking them for help. Explain that you have tried fixing the problem before asking them for help. Then, take note when they explain things to you and try to follow their directions closely. Depending on your child, you may also ask them additional questions now. Don't use this as an opportunity to lecture your child or invade their privacy while they are helping you. Instead, use this opportunity to foster open communication and mutual learning.

Step 5: Be Respectful of Your Child's Privacy and Respect Their Boundaries

Whenever you are using a shared social media platform with your child, you must respect their boundaries while doing so. For example, if your child doesn't like it when you comment on all their stories or share their content on your platforms, you must respect it. Even if you feel like they are being unreasonable, you must remember that they are in an emotionally vulnerable stage of life. If you overstep their boundaries, they might lash out or simply won't trust you anymore. This could result in them not wishing to share anything else with you.

Step 6: Discuss Any Dangers You Come Across on Social Media With Your Child (The Power of Anecdotes)

As you become more familiar with the social media platform, you may encounter several potentially dangerous situations. For example, you may encounter strangers wishing to communicate with you, scams, or inappropriate content. This is the perfect opportunity to teach your child about the importance of online safety. Again, approaching the situation the right way is crucial. Instead of approaching it like a lecture and laying down the rules for your child, approach it as a story or anecdote instead. Have a conversation with your child about your social media experience and ask if they have ever had a similar experience.

Then, share some tips or safety measures you think they can use should they ever encounter a similar situation. This approach can help you discuss important safety protocols with your child without making them feel like you are lecturing them. It can also provide an opportunity for your child to share any dangerous or scary experiences they have had on social media, and you can guide them on how they should handle these situations in the future.

Step 7: Keep an Open Mind When Using Social Media

When using social media, it's easy to obsess over the negative aspects and potential dangers. However, doing so will not help you or your child. It is, therefore, important that you keep an open mind when using social media. While there are a lot of negative or potentially dangerous situations on social media, you must focus on the positive ones instead. Furthermore, if you come across potentially dangerous factors on social media, discuss these with your child, explaining why and how you think they are dangerous and what you expect your child to do if they encounter them. Bear in mind that there is a generational gap between you and most users on the platform. This might lead you to think that certain topics are inappropriate or strange when they aren't for the younger generation. This is yet another reason why open communication is so important.

Step 8: Show Your Child That You Trust Them

Finally, while it might be easy to operate like a helicopter parent and monitor your child's every move on social media, you must show them you trust them and give them the benefit of the doubt. Instead of asking, "Have you been using XYZ website?" or "I hope you aren't giving your personal information to strangers on the internet," have an open discussion with them, explaining why they shouldn't do these things (and that it's for their safety). Then, trust that they will act responsibly and come to you if they should ever feel threatened, in danger, or hurt by something that happened on social media.

As mentioned before, if you prohibit your child from exploring social media platforms, they will end up resenting you and will start keeping secrets and acting behind your back. Therefore, you must make them feel like they can trust you by trusting them. As a parent, this is a difficult but necessary step for fostering mutual learning, trust, respect, and openness.

An Open-Door Policy: Creating a Safe Space for Digital Dialogues

Speaking of openness, now might be the perfect time to introduce an open-door policy in your home. This policy can create a safe space for discussions about social media, online activities, and other important topics, including bullying, relationships, and the importance of privacy. If you don't know what an open-door policy is or what it entails, you are about to find out. In this section, we'll discuss everything you should know about it to help you foster a closer relationship with your child while ensuring you offer them the support and protection they need from social media. So, what is an open-door policy, and how does it work?

What is an Open-Door Policy

An open-door policy is a policy that allows for open communication between parents and their children. Schools, kindergartens, and workplaces have started implementing open-door policies to make life easier for children, parents, employees, and employers alike. Essentially, an open-door policy is a policy that states that you are always available to your child or employee when needed. For example, if an open-door policy is implemented at work, it allows employees to communicate their needs and requests directly with their manager whenever they need to. Instead of making an appointment with their team leader, manager, or boss, they can pop into their office anytime and discuss what is bothering them.

An open-door policy at home allows for the same thing. Instead of having a physical door that is always open, you declare that you are always open and available for your child whenever they need you. I know most parents think that they automatically have an open-door policy with their children. However, that's not always the case. If your child feels that you will scold or judge them when they come to you with a problem, they might not feel comfortable doing so. In this case, they don't interpret you as having an open-door policy with them. Furthermore, if your open-door policy always ends with them getting punished, they won't come to you with their problems.

An open-door policy is not the same as forcing your child to confess when taking a cookie. It is meant to be a safe space where your child feels comfortable sharing something with you. It can be something that happened to them on social media, at school, or at a friend's house. It can also be something they know they did wrong and now need your help to fix. Implementing an open-door policy at home takes some hard work on both sides, patience, and dedication from both parties. We'll discuss some tips for introducing an open-door policy at home in the following section. However, before we do so, it's important to consider the pros and cons of this policy.

Depending on your relationship with your children, you may feel more or less comfortable with this arrangement. Because for the time the open-door policy is in play, you are not acting as a parent (someone with authority) but a confidant. That affects how you are allowed to react when your child tells you something. This might be a more challenging exercise for some, especially if you are used to a very traditional child-parent relationship where children are meant to be seen and not heard.

Advantages of an Open-Door Policy

There are many advantages of an open-door policy. In the workplace, it allows employees to have a closer connection with their colleagues and managers, and managers can deal with issues at work much faster than if there were not an open-door policy. The same is true at home. If you want a strong connection with your child or if you want your child to feel that they can come to you for anything, an open-door policy really is the best way to achieve that. Here are some specific advantages of an open-door policy relating to social media between a parent and child.

It Makes Your Child Feel Supported

If you assure your child that you are always available to them, no matter what they are going through, they will feel supported and loved. This increases the chances of them coming to you if they have a problem, which is crucial if you want to foster a deep connection with your child. Encouraging your child to tell you about their day, no matter how trivial, will make them feel like you really care about their emotional well-being. In a world that gets as busy as it does, it's important that your child feels you care about their emotional needs as well as their physical well-being. An open-door policy can help accomplish this.

You Will Feel a Greater Sense of Peace

If your child feels comfortable talking to you, they are likely to share with you. This can increase your sense of peace, as you know they will come to you if anything bad happens. By making time daily to talk about their day, how they are doing, and anything else they would like to share, you will feel more connected with them, and you can pick up when something is bothering them. Whether it's social media or at school, you will know that your child will talk to you if anything is bothering them or if something is wrong.

You Can Help Your Child Through a Crisis

An open-door policy can help you feel more connected with your child. It can also enable you to help them through a crisis. If they feel comfortable talking to you, they are likely to come to you if something bad happens. This allows you to guide them through the crises and offer them the support they need. For example, if your child comes to you explaining that they have been the victim of online bullying, you can guide them through this situation by helping them cope with the emotional stress it causes and guiding them on how they can respond.

An open-door policy creates room for better communication and allows you to help your child manage the normal and abnormal parts of growing up in the digital age.

Challenges of an Open-Door Policy

While there are advantages of an open-door policy, there are also some challenges, especially if you are not used to having such open communication with your child. As a parent, you only want the best for your child, which might come with some uncomfortable situations to manage. An open-door policy requires patience and mutual trust from both you and your child. These are some of the most common challenges you may face when introducing an open-door policy.

You Have to Keep Your Composure

When your child comes to you with a problem, their situation may be embarrassing, or they might be in trouble because they did something foolish or against your house rules. However, the purpose of an open-door policy is to promote open communication between you and your child. That means you cannot react emotionally when your child comes to you with a problem. Regardless of the situation, it's important that you keep your composure and remain objective. Listen while your child is talking, and carefully consider how you react. Furthermore, you must carefully consider what actions to take in this situation so you don't embarrass your child or make them feel uncomfortable.

You Cannot Punish Your Child in the Moment

While you may be infuriated when your child explains their situation (especially if they are in trouble for doing something you told them not to do), it's crucial that you keep an open mind and not punish them at that moment. Doing this will only worsen the situation. It can make your child feel embarrassed, or they might regret coming to you in the first place. That doesn't mean you cannot enforce the repercussions of breaking the rules. However, this is not the time to do so. While you can discuss punishment later, what you need to do when your child comes to you is listen to them and try to find a solution for the problem, no matter how upset you are.

You Cannot Break Your Child's Trust

Regardless of how mad or upset you are with your child, you cannot break their trust. As a parent, we want to jump on the situation and get it sorted. Sometimes, that means going to the authorities, confronting another parent, seeing the principal at school, or any other action you deem necessary based on the situation. However, if your child feels embarrassed about the situation already, they might ask you not to do anything about it. This is an extremely difficult situation to navigate, as you may feel strongly that additional action is required (especially if your child is in danger). But even if you feel something should be done, you cannot break your child's trust in the process.

Instead of doing what you think is best regardless of their feelings, discuss the matter with them and explain why you feel the actions you will take are necessary. Then, reassure them that you are acting in their best interest and that their well-being is your priority. Ensure your child understands that you are not angry with them (even if you are) and that you are grateful they came to you with their problem. This will ensure your child keeps trusting you and prevents them from withdrawing in the future.

How to Introduce an Open-Door Policy at Home

Introducing an open-door policy at home might feel strange at first, especially if you are not used to having such open communication with your child. Furthermore, they might not be comfortable sharing certain parts of their life with you. This policy can be a huge help if they are ever in trouble, especially if the trouble relates to social media, where you cannot control their environment or what they are exposed to. The earlier you introduce the open-door policy, the better. Younger children are more inclined to share with their parents, especially regarding social media information.

Introducing an open-door policy before they start using technology and social media is ideal, as this allows you to safely explain the rules and guidelines for using these platforms. However, if your child is older, you can still introduce this idea to them. You must explain to your child what you mean by an open-door policy: that you are always available to them and that you will be patient and attentive when they come to you. Sometimes, a symbolic object might be useful, especially if your child has difficulty opening up to you because they fear they will be in trouble.

For example, you could give your child a physical object (such as a shell, candle, or toy) that they can hold when telling you about something that happened. You can name this object "The talking […]." Whoever has the talking object at that time is the only one allowed to speak. This ensures that everyone gets equal speaking time. It also allows you to listen intently when your child speaks and gives you time to compose yourself before responding.

In addition to a talking object, you can assign a specific area in your home for open-door discussions. This way, you will know what to expect when your child asks if they can see you in that area, and you can prepare yourself for a more serious talk with them. Since each family structure is different, these tools may work for you, or they might not work for you. Experimenting with different ways to incorporate the open-door policy in your home and asking your child for their input, can make the experience more engaging and help everyone feel comfortable sharing their thoughts and feelings. Introducing an open-door policy might take some time and patience, but it will be worth it when you can rest assured that your child will come to you if they ever need anything.

Screen Savvy: Strategies for Staying Informed About Your Child's Online World

When your child was small and you were younger, you likely thought that you would always be up to date with the apps and platforms they would use. Now, however, you may feel like you cannot stay ahead. Just when you get used to one platform, they start using another. Staying up to date with what they are using and what they are using it for can feel like a never-ending battle. But you may find it crucial to have at least some idea of which social media platforms they are using and why.

Ask Your Child About It

A reminder of a suggestion that we made earlier in this chapter: The best way to learn about a social media platform is to ask someone who uses it frequently, in this case, that person is your child. A casual discussion about the new social media platform your child is using and what the platform is for can give you a better idea of whether it is something you should worry about. It gives you some insight into what your child is currently interested in. Most children will not mind explaining the basics of what a social media platform is and how it is used by their parents. Try not to be judgmental when your child explains what a platform is, as this might discourage them from opening up in the future.

Asking your child about a social media platform has another advantage—it can tell you if there is something you should really be worried about. Very few children can successfully lie to their parents, especially when asked a direct question. Therefore, if you ask your child about a social media platform and they don't want to tell you the basics of how it works or what it is used for, you can take it as a sign that they are most likely using it for something they should not be using it for. Whether they are talking to strangers online, sharing personal information, or viewing inappropriate content, your child will not wish to share this information with you if they know they are engaging in poor behavior.

As always, anecdotes work excellently when you are trying to get your child to engage in a conversation without making it seem like you are questioning them. You can tell them that you saw an advertisement about a social media platform, read about the platform on one of your *Facebook* groups, or heard one of their friends' parents discussing the platform. Then, you can ask them if they have ever heard of it or know how it works. As always, sounding interested instead of accusatory will get you a long way in terms of discussing the platform. Your child might even be excited to show you how it works.

Watch YouTube Videos and Tutorials

Another way to learn more about a social media platform and how it works is by watching YouTube tutorials. Whenever a new app or product is released, someone will publish a video reviewing it or sharing information about it. Sometimes, it is the design company themselves. Other times, it might be a third party. In any case, you will likely find some interesting information on YouTube about the social media platform. There, you can learn the platform's intended use and how children use it in real life. Because, let's be honest, people don't always use online platforms for their intended purposes.

When watching a YouTube tutorial, you may already understand the potential risks associated with that platform. These risks may include scams, predators, or space to see inappropriate content. Even the most innocent platforms can be used and abused by online users, turning the platform into something it was never created for in the first place. Some YouTube videos may discuss certain risks associated with online platforms, while other videos might give you more information on the various ways in which this platform can be used.

Watching a YouTube tutorial or other "how to" video will give you a great idea of what this platform is intended for, why your child may be using it, and who the intended audience is. Be careful with which videos you watch, though. Remember that many people make videos to push a certain agenda. You may watch one tutorial explaining the pros and cons while another video exclusively talks about the advantages and uses of the platform, making it seem like there are no potential risks in using it. It's better to be open-minded when researching a social media platform and consider the uses of the platform from all angles.

Research the Common Dangers

Having said that, it is also worth considering the dangers of a certain platform. Many online websites, and as mentioned, YouTube tutorials will discuss potential ways in which a platform can be misused or how it might be dangerous for children. Your child's age and emotional maturity will also factor into which dangers they are at risk for. For example, if a social media platform has many users pushing the sale of their products, your child might be vulnerable to being influenced by these people, leading them to spend money on things they don't need.

Or, the social media platform might have specific users or companies that promote dangerous things, such as drug use, pornography, or online dating. Online dating is fine if you are an adult, but a child might be convinced to meet someone behind your back, leading them to a potentially dangerous situation. Therefore, it is worth researching the common dangers associated with an online platform. What you consider to be a danger depends on your child and what you consider to be dangerous. Some dangers will differ depending on your religious or cultural background.

When you come across potential or known threats, the best thing to do is to note them and discuss them with your child at an appropriate time. Again, anecdotes or stories can be beneficial for opening a discussion without sounding accusatory. Whether your child believes you or shares your concerns about a platform or not is irrelevant. Teaching them about online safety and explaining the risks and repercussions of using a platform for dangerous activities is crucial and forms part of your parental experience. If you notice that a platform has too many risks or the risks are too prevalent on the platform, you might have to prohibit your child from using it. I know that's easier said than done, but explaining why you don't want your child using a platform can help them understand the risks, and they might come to the same conclusion themselves.

Try the Platform Yourself

While I've previously said you don't have to use every platform your child uses, the best way to learn about a platform (including its potential risks) is by using it. Trying the platform yourself will equip you with everything you need to understand how the platform works and really get the hang of it. Using the platform—even if it's just for a few days—will also notify you of any potential risks. For example, you may notice that the algorithm sends a lot of body-related content your way, such as fitness inspiration, diets, and exercise models. This might trigger teenagers, especially if they already struggle with body confidence problems.

Furthermore, you can see how easy it is for others to gain your personal information or communicate with you. Some platforms require that you first accept a message request before you can talk to a person. Other platforms don't have this feature, meaning anyone who wants to can talk to you whenever they see fit. This is another potential danger of a platform and something you should discuss with your child in order to teach them how to manage it if a situation like this occurs. You can also judge what most of the content on the platform is about if you use it yourself. This can give you a better sense of whether it is an appropriate platform for your children.

While it might be excessive to install and try out every platform your children use, it could be the best way to determine if the platform is appropriate for your children and if there are any serious risks involved with using it. Remember that the risks aren't always physical, but can be emotionally damaging as well, increasing the risk of mental health conditions, low self-esteem, and self-harm. If you feel that the platform has too much negative content, it is worth discussing with your child why they want to use it and considering whether there are any alternatives or which methods you will follow to keep them safe.

Key Takeaway From Chapter 3

In this extensive chapter, we discussed how you can become a digital chaperone and effectively protect your children from the dangers of social media while giving them the freedom needed to explore the various platforms. This takes patience and dedication. We discussed crossing the digital threshold and promoting honest communication with your child. We also discussed the advantages of a family contract regarding social media use. Since you might not be as clued up about the different social media platforms as your children are, we discussed eight steps for promoting mutual learning to enable you to understand the platforms better and help your child.

We also considered the advantages and challenges of an open-door policy and how to introduce such a policy to your home so your child always knows they can come to you in a time of need. Finally, we discovered how you could become more tech-savvy and learn more about the social media platforms your child is using, identifying the risks of each platform, and enabling yourself to guide your children on the path to responsible social media use.

Chapter 4:

The Power of Digital Resilience

Being a good parent requires knowing when to push and when to back off. When to help and when to let them make mistakes. And then be strong enough to watch them go. —Anonymous

Letting your children go and giving them more freedom can be tough for any parent, especially considering all the dangers in the world. When they are small, your children rely on you for everything. They rely on you to make them food, to choose their clothes, to read them a bedtime story, and to wake them up for school. But when they become older, they rely on you less and less. And while no parent would argue that having two hands for yourself is something to celebrate, giving your child the independence they seek can be difficult.

Yet giving them more independence and gradually letting go of your control over them is a crucial and natural part of watching them grow up. If you have a close connection with your child, you can rest assured that they will be responsible and come to you if they ever have a problem. But there is another way you can ensure your child is prepared for this world. That's by teaching them about resilience. Resilience is an important skill for all phases in life.

Digital resilience is becoming increasingly important as children become more involved with various aspects of digital media. This chapter will discuss the power of digital resilience and how you can introduce this concept to your child and teach them about digital resilience.

Building Blocks: The Concept of Digital Resilience

Your children will start learning about resilience from a young age. Resilience is the ability to recover from difficulties. Mya Patel describes resilience brilliantly in her book, *The Resilient Woman*. She says the following, "Imagine a rubber band. It can be stretched, pulled, and twisted, but it always returns to its original shape. That, in essence, is resilience" (Patel, n.d.).

Children learn resilience by facing obstacles. When young, they must learn to dress, tie their shoes, and be good at school. When they get older, their challenges become more difficult. They must learn to face rejection, failure, and bullying at school. Being resilient and having a thick skin is crucial today, and any teenager will testify to it. As Ginsburg and FitzGerald (2011) explain in their book, *Letting Go With Love and Confidence*, "When adolescents are resilient, they aren't invulnerable, but they are equipped to handle change and rebound from adversity, rather than feeling victimized and hopeless."

The art of resilience becomes increasingly important the older your child gets. If they don't know how to deal with loss or rejection, they will fall apart every time they are faced with it, and they won't be mentally strong enough to handle life as an adult. Therefore, it's important that you gradually give them more freedom as they age while ensuring they are resilient enough to handle the challenges life will undoubtedly throw their way. Teaching them to be resilient is important for every aspect of their lives. And now, teaching them about digital resilience is becoming even more important.

We'll discuss the effects of online bullying in Chapter 6. However, it is important to mention that digital resilience is about more than resisting online bullies. It's also about recovering from things your children are exposed to on digital platforms. Despite your best efforts, you cannot protect your children 100% from being exposed to horrors online. People wearing cameras strapped to their chests while shooting a mosque full of people, pornography, and racial and moral debates are merely some of the content your children may be exposed to online.

As we have established before, prohibiting your child from using social media certainly is not the answer. But what else can you do? You can teach them how to use digital technology safely. You can also teach them how to be resilient using digital platforms so they aren't as susceptible to the sad and terrifying information circling the internet. Digital resilience also protects them against falling prey to websites like the Blue Whale Challenge, which could potentially save their lives. Furthermore, digital resilience can protect your child's mental health.

While many useful and wonderful things are online, there are also many heartbreaking and horrifying stories. My Facebook is flooded with stories of people who have abandoned their dogs in plastic bags near sewers, leaving them for dead. Every day, when your child uses social media, they will potentially be exposed to these things. While these are facts of life and these events do occur, your child's mental and emotional health could suffer if they are constantly exposed to this type of content. They don't even have to go searching to find it.

Digital resilience will also prevent children from falling prey to online predators or scams. While many people share good news, useful tips, and help children become inspiring people, some exploit the youth—either to make a quick buck from their innocence or use them for their own needs and desires. Teaching your child about digital resilience can improve their resistance to these types of people and help them use digital platforms safely and wisely.

Building digital resilience is not restricted to your children. You will also need to learn some digital resilience. Building digital resilience can help you with your resilience overall. For example, if you are more resilient to what people say about you online, you will also become more resilient to what they say in person. Building digital resilience allows you to better equip your children for the world they are heading into. This world can be scary and cruel, and it may feel like the world is out to hurt your child. While you cannot shield them from all the dangers they will face along the way, you can prepare them for it by helping them become more resilient, resourceful, and mentally strong.

While resilience, in general, is not a new concept, digital resilience is. That's why you must understand the potential threats your child will face in the world. It is the only way to help them prepare for it and to help you feel more secure when letting them go out into the world. In the following section, we will discover how to foster digital resilience while protecting your child as much as possible and protecting their mental health.

Shielding the Psyche, Nurturing Resilience

Now that you understand why digital resilience is so important for anyone using digital technology, we will discover how to build it. Building digital resilience is not like building resilience in the real world. Most of a child's resilience in the real world comes from real experiences and trial and error. Falling out of a tree, falling off their bikes, burning their mouths when eating too-hot food. These things show them that there are consequences for their actions and teach them not only resilience but also to make smarter decisions.

Unfortunately, we don't want our children to learn from experience when it comes to digital resilience. We don't want to expose them to the elements that force them to become resilient, as these elements are dangerous and can be damaging to their mental health and their psyche. According to *Good Therapy*, "The psyche refers to all of the elements of the human mind, both conscious and unconscious," (*Psyche*, 2013). The psyche is also often used to describe a person's emotional well-being.

Therefore, to protect our children's psyche, we must find different ways of teaching them about digital safety and digital resilience without exposing them to the factors that call for it. An article in *Computers and Education Open* discussed the effects of educational and parent intervention in nurturing digital resilience in elementary school children. This article mentions the following, "The intervention improved students' digital skills, self-efficacy with technology, intentions of being an upstander to support peers online, and willingness to seek help for difficult situations from trusted adults" (Lee & Hancock, 2023).

This proves how invaluable parent and caretaker intervention is regarding digital resilience. It is our responsibility as their guardians to protect them against the elements that are out to harm them. But we are also responsible for preparing them to face these dangers alone when they leave our homes. However, as we have already established, we are somewhat out of our depth here, as we have not grown up with digital technology. Teaching children about digital resilience is, therefore, much more challenging. According to the *Computers and Education Open* study, we should focus on a few core aspects when nurturing digital resilience in our children. These aspects are as follows.

The Concept of Digital Resilience

The first area you should be focusing on is explaining what digital resilience is and why they need it. Helping your child understand the risks of digital technology allows you to help them navigate these platforms safely and with more care. Explaining that they might come across dangerous situations and then need to be resilient enough to overcome these threats is crucial if you want your child to understand the risks of digital technology and be vigilant. Furthermore, the more your child understands what digital resilience is, the better they will develop a problem-solving strategy. This way, they can take charge and not become a victim of the problem.

Developing Digital Skills

Another area you should focus on when nurturing digital resilience is allowing your child to develop their digital skills. It's true that with more digital skills comes riskier online behavior, but it's also true that children will need to have some digital skills if they want to know how to use these digital platforms safely. We will discuss later how to help your child develop their digital skills without following a trial-and-error route that could lead to dangerous situations.

Self-Efficacy When Using Technology

While you may think that the best way to protect your child from the threats posed by digital technology is to monitor them at all times, that is not practical or a viable solution. Instead, children must learn how to use these digital technologies by themselves. Studies have shown that children are more resilient to cyberbullying and other online threats when they feel more confident that they can stand up for themselves (Lee & Hancock, 2023).

Supporting Others

A study in OFCOM, the UK's official communication regulator, found the following (*Children and Parents*, 2023):

> Children's use of social media in proactively positive ways has decreased over the past year. For example, fewer had sent supportive messages to friends who were having a hard time (51% in 2022 vs 61% in 2021). This behavioral shift was in evidence among our Children's Media Lives participants, who were using online communications platforms more for viewing content than for actively engaging with friends. (p. 3)

Yet another factor you should focus on when nurturing digital resilience in your child is the importance of supporting others. If your child sees a friend or peer being bullied online, or if one of their friends comes to them asking for help with a crisis, your child should be able to help and support them. If children are encouraged to support each other and stand up to cyberbullies with their friends, they will be more resilient and confident in navigating the digital world.

Seeking Help

Finally, as discussed previously, children need to understand when to seek help when they are in trouble online. While they should have a sense of self-efficacy, they should also understand that when things become too much for them to handle (or in the case of online predators), they should come to you or an adult for help. Ensuring they understand that you will not be mad with them and you will help them through the problem is crucial to nurturing digital resilience in your child.

How to Teach Children About Digital Resilience

Considering the factors above, it is time to discuss the steps for nurturing digital resilience in your child while still protecting their psyche. Unfortunately, unlike with many other situations, you cannot entirely just allow your child to "try and see." Instead, you must lay the groundwork that helps them become more digitally resilient. Explaining the dangers of digital technology alone is not enough. You also need to be involved with their development online and ensure they are resilient enough to overcome the threats they may face in the digital world. Here are 8 steps for fostering digital resilience in your child without exposing them to mentally damaging content or experiences.

Step 1: Build an Honest Relationship

We've discussed the importance of building an open and honest relationship with your child. It is the first step in helping them understand the importance of online safety. It is also a crucial part of fostering digital resilience, as they must know that they can come to you if they are ever in trouble. Building an open, honest relationship with your child starts when they are young. Teaching them core values, such as knowing right from wrong, is also important in this scenario, as it helps them understand when bad things are happening online and encourages them to come to you when this happens.

I also believe it's important for us parents to work on ourselves if we want to effectively support our children. We, as parents, often let our emotions dictate our actions during challenging situations involving our children. However, if we want to build an honest relationship with them, we must work on ourselves as well. We must become adaptable and flexible, manage our emotions, and learn from our mistakes. This is the only way to effectively help our children.

Step 2: Foster Digital Skills

As mentioned in the previous section, you cannot expect your child to become digitally resilient without digital skills. Instead, you must allow them to explore the uses and benefits of digital technology. If you are open about using this technology, they are also likely to come to you if they have a problem, especially since they won't use it behind your back. Encouraging safe and appropriate online use is a crucial step for showing your child that while there are dangers and threats online, there are also many benefits to understanding how digital technology works.

Step 3: Allow Appropriate Engagement

One way to encourage your child's digital skills is by allowing for age-appropriate engagement. There are so many different digital sources for children of all ages. For example, toddlers can learn to watch their favorite shows on a streaming site while you explain the importance of asking you before watching something new. This helps them understand that not all shows and platforms are safe for them to use. Older children may have more online freedom, but it's still important to explain your expectations and what you don't want them to use digital technology for, and why.

Step 4: Encourage Self-Sufficiency and Problem-Solving

This is another reason why encouraging digital use from a young age is beneficial in building digital resilience. It allows you to encourage your child to become more self-sufficient. For example, if your child doesn't know how to search for their favorite show, you can help them navigate the platform while explaining some of the risks. By allowing your children to explore digital technology in a controlled environment, they get some experience without being exposed to the threats on the platform. It also helps to develop their problem-solving skills, which is useful in every aspect of their lives.

Step 5: Set a Good Example

Children often copy our behavior. You may notice this when doing daily tasks, such as holding your spoon when eating breakfast, sighing when listening to the news, and interacting with other people. Children will, therefore, also model your online behavior. Suppose you always talk about negative aspects of social media, leave nasty comments on other people's posts, and engage in risky online behavior, like talking to strangers online or watching pornography. In that case, your child is likely also to model this behavior.

Step 6: Send a Positive Message About Digital Technology

Part of setting a good example is being positive about digital technology. While it is important to discuss the risks of the online world with your child, it is equally important that you help them understand the many advantages of it. Digital technology offers new methods of communication, learning opportunities, and the chance to experience new and wonderful things they would not experience without it. Therefore, you must help them understand digital technology's benefits and useful aspects, ensuring they understand that it is a positive tool overall.

Step 7: Recognize Learning Opportunities

It's also important that you and your child recognize the learning opportunities available on digital platforms. If your child understands what they stand to gain from digital technology, they will be more open when using it. They will understand and respect the potential risks of the online world without fearing it. Have you ever seen prey when they suspect they are being hunted? They immediately change their demeanor and essentially put a bigger target on their back. If your child is naive about the threats of digital technology, or if they are too cautious to familiarize themselves with how a platform works and the potential threats, they run a greater risk of falling prey to the dangers of it.

But suppose you can help them understand that there are so many opportunities to grow and learn on various digital platforms. In that case, they are likely to use these platforms for educational and other positive opportunities rather than negative ones.

Step 8: Use Interactive Social Technologies

Interactive social technologies, like multiplayer games (*Fortnite, Apex Legends, League of Legends, Minecraft,* and more), can teach children from a young age how to behave online. It teaches them about communication, empathy, and regulating their own emotions. It also teaches them how to behave if they don't win the game or have their way. Therefore, digital resilience can also help your child improve their character and resilience in real life. It's important that you, as a parent, follow these steps and help your child discover the digital world safely but also independently.

Reflections and Pauses

In Chapter 2 we discussed some case studies and examples of where social media use led to mental health conditions among teenagers. Their stories were chilling, and the statistics shared in that chapter about the number of children and teenagers suffering from mental health conditions that are exacerbated by social media may have left you scared and worried for your child's health. However, by teaching your child digital resilience, you can help them overcome these obstacles. Let's now consider a few case studies of children who were also in danger through digital technology use but overcame the danger by using the digital resilience skills they have acquired.

Case Study #1: Raz's Story

Raz was a girl who enjoyed meeting people online. She lived in a small town and had a few friends at her school, but she didn't really have a shared interest with many of these friends. She found many like-minded people online and enjoyed sharing her thoughts and experiences with these people. One day, Raz met a person called Brad online. He shared many of Raz's interests and said he was 12 years old, which was the same age as Raz. The two of them talked, and then Brad suggested they meet somewhere close to her house.

He told her that she shouldn't tell her parents, as they would probably not allow them to meet. He also asked for her address so he could meet her somewhere close to home; a safe place. But Raz knew better. Her parents had taught her to never to give away personal information online. She also felt uneasy when talking to Brad, as he asked many personal questions. When Raz told her parents about her encounter, they read through the chats and discovered that Brad was not a 12-year-old boy but likely an online predator.

Case Study #2: Ben's Predicament

Ben joined Facebook at 12. He enjoyed talking with people around the world about all sorts of topics. Unfortunately, Ben wasn't careful when using Facebook and often posted personal information, like where he likes to go after school and his telephone number, should anyone want to call him. Ben and his friends also created a fake Facebook account that they used to tease other kids at school. They picked on one kid who lived with his grandmother after his parents abandoned him. Later, the school found out about what Ben and his friends had been up to, and they were in a lot of trouble because of it.

That's not all. Ben started getting strange phone calls from a man wanting to meet him so they could discuss some of the things Ben shared online. Ben also noticed a strange man hanging around his house after school. Eventually, although he was scared, Ben told his father what had happened. Ben knew that although his father might have been mad at him, he would still help Ben. Although his father was mad at Ben, he managed his emotions and showed restraint in the moment. He called the police and detained the strange man for following Ben. They also removed his Facebook account, and all the personal information shared on the platform was erased.

Case Study #3: Mark's Trouble

Mark (14) enjoys playing video games just as much as the next kid. However, his gaming habits got out of control, and his school work suffered for it. When Mark realized he had an essay due that he did not have time to finish because he was playing games the whole time, he used an AI generator to plagiarize the essay. He got away with it once and started doing this with all his essays. It wasn't until exam time that Mark's teachers noticed that things were not quite as they seemed. As if that's not bad enough. One of Mark's friends showed him how to download video games illegally, and Mark decided to download a game rated for players 18 years and older.

Mark also used his mother's credit card to pay for some of the games he bought online. One of these games turned out to be a scam, and his mother lost a lot of money in the process. Thereafter, Mark's mother had a stern talk with him, reminding him why his actions were wrong and how they could put him in danger. She also reminded him that the games he was playing, especially those with a higher age restriction, were not appropriate and that they could harm his mental health.

Case Study #4: Becky's Story

Becky is 15 years old and recently broke up with her boyfriend, Todd. Their relationship was never good, and Becky's parents disapproved of Todd, but the relationship ended after Todd was caught cheating on Becky. Although Becky ended the relationship and said that she never wanted to see Todd again, he did not leave her alone. He would follow her around school and take pictures of her. He then sent these pictures and other inappropriate content to her when she was at home. Becky started feeling afraid that Todd would try to hurt her.

Fortunately, Becky had a close relationship with her aunt, whom she told about her experience with Todd. Together, Becky and her aunt explained the situation to her parents, who were grateful that Becky went to an adult with her concerns. They helped Becky handle the situation and prohibited Todd from contacting her again.

Case Study #5: Hassan's Online Troubles

Hassan was an immigrant student in a new school in America. He was well-liked by his classmates despite being from abroad. Given Hassan's foreign origins, he was always caring for exchange students and new students in general. So, when Rashmi, a foreign exchange student, entered his class, Hassan was generous and kind towards her. They also became friends online and often discussed things they found interesting about America online. Soon after Rashmi entered Hassan's school, she was being bullied by other kids in the class for having a funny accent.

The bullying followed her home as the kids also made fun of her online. Hassan would not stand for this, however. He quickly confronted the bullies and put them in their place. He also took the matter to his school's principal, explaining that he would not allow another foreign student to be picked on for being different. Hassan showed digital resilience and stood up for a classmate, helping her in the process.

These are all good examples of how children build digital resilience and how this resilience is beneficial for their health and safety. Following the steps in the previous section will ensure your child has the resilience needed to operate the digital world safely and confidently.

Key Takeaway From Chapter 4

This chapter focused on nurturing digital resilience in children. Digital resilience is the ability to withstand and overcome challenges in the digital world. These challenges include cyberbullying, inappropriate content, scams, and other factors that endanger your child's physical and mental well-being. To foster digital resilience in a child, you must focus on five aspects: the concept of digital resilience, developing digital skills, self-efficacy when using digital platforms, supporting others, and seeking help.

We shared eight steps for fostering digital resilience in children. They include building an honest relationship with your child, fostering digital skills, allowing appropriate online engagement, encouraging online problem-solving, setting a good example, sending a positive message about digital technology, recognizing learning opportunities, and using interactive social technologies. We also discussed five case studies that show how children use the digital resilience they have acquired for online safety.

Nurturing digital resilience in your child is equipping them with a shield designed to stop all digital 'bullets'.

Chapter 5:

Finding Balance in the Digital Era

Regardless of how well prepared your child is for facing the online world, it's still important to teach them about balance in this digital era. Balancing your online time may be something you struggle with as well. It's extremely easy to become addicted to social media. It's just as easy to isolate yourself from the world around you, including the people you love, because you are so busy online. But it doesn't have to be that way. Teaching your children to balance their online time is a crucial factor for raising well-rounded, balanced children who can manage their time well.

This chapter will help you navigate the online world and find balance between time online and time in the real world. Finding a healthy balance between the two is crucial, and although you might not be their favorite parent when invoking a screen-free time rule, it will surely benefit them in the long-term. So, let's see how you can find equilibrium between online and offline time.

Striking Harmony: Offline—Online Equilibrium

Being connected to the digital world has pros and cons, as we have established in the previous chapter. But regardless of how many positive elements there are in the digital world, being connected to it 24/7 is not a good idea. In fact, there are several mental and physical problems that can stem from too much time online. Mental problems that often arise from too much screen time include:

- Withdrawal from those around you

- Anger

- Depression

- Tension

- Irritability

- Restlessness

- Losing your sense of time as you spend all day on the phone

- Loss of productivity

- Lower grades in school.

- Fallouts with friends and family

- Personality changes

In addition to these troublesome effects that too much time on digital media may have on you and your child's mental health, it can also lead to physical problems, including:

- **Neck problems:** Looking down toward your screen all day can lead to neck pain and poor posture.

- **Eye strain:** Staring at a small screen for prolonged periods may lead to headaches, burning eyes, blurred vision, and eye strain. It might result in needing prescription glasses to repair the damage caused by the screen.

- **Increased illness:** When you aren't spending enough time exercising and being outside, your immune system can take a plunge. Furthermore, phones are covered in bacteria and germs that can make you sick.

- **Loss of concentration:** If you are addicted to digital technology, you may not be able to focus, even when you aren't using it. This increases your risk for car accidents and other dangerous situations caused by a lack of concentration.

- **Reduced fertility:** Preliminary studies have shown that the signals emitted from a cell phone may reduce sperm motility and sperm count (*Signs and Symptoms of Cell Phone Addiction*, 2013). The effects of cell phone use on female fertility is not yet confirmed, but it may affect female fertility as well.

Considering the negative effects that can arise from spending too much time on digital technology, you can see that it is important to find balance between online and offline time. We'll discuss some strategies for introducing offline time in the following section. For now, however, let's consider some of the benefits your child could gain from having a balance between the time he spends online and offline.

Spending Time Offline Provides More Time for Other Activities

If your child spends less time online, they will have more time available for other activities. This could be studying, spending time with loved ones, or practicing a hobby. It's important that your child has hobbies outside of the ones they have online. Allowing them to learn a new skill or do something relaxing or enjoyable when they are not online helps them to develop a better understanding of the uses and limitations of digital technology and gives them a healthier balance between online and offline time. Of course, it also means they will have more time for homework, so they are less likely to fall behind in school.

Screen Time is Seen as a Reward for Good Behavior

Another advantage of having set online and offline times is that your child views screen time as a reward. Whether it's a reward for good behavior, or a nice treat after finishing all their homework and chores for the day, having screen time as a treat instead of 24/7 access helps your child realize that they don't need to be connected to their phones all the time. It also helps them realize the intended purpose of social media platforms and online games—they are meant to entertain you and not fill up all your time.

The Brain Sees Digital Time as a Reward

Have you ever heard of a dopamine detox? Dopamine is the hormone secreted by the brain that increases your mood and makes you feel euphoric. It's the same hormone released during exercise that makes you feel great after a workout. However, the more time you spend scrolling mindlessly online, the less sensitive your brain becomes to rewards. It no longer views screen time as a reward and therefore doesn't release dopamine. However, if your child sees screen time as a reward, their brain will also do so, and it will start releasing dopamine when they are online, improving their mood and reducing the risk of depression.

Refer to Illustrations A and B for a visual depiction of how social media use affects your child's mental health. **Illustration A** depicts how the dopamine depletion caused by continuous social media usage results in poor mental health for your child. **Illustration B** shows how the temporary deprivation of social media will result in dopamine recalibration and improved mental health. The illustrations are provided at the end of this chapter.

Your Child Has Better Social Skills

Another problem with too much online time is that children no longer learn how to communicate with others effectively. If they are on their phones even when spending time with friends and family, they will lose valuable communication time. They won't develop the same social skills as they would if they were not permanently connected to their phones. Therefore, a child with a better balance between online and offline time will also have better social skills.

Your Child is Not at Risk of Becoming Addicted to Digital Technology

Finally, your child will not be at risk for becoming addicted to social media or digital technology if they don't have access to it all the time. As parents, we should not let the attraction our child has for digital technology become an addiction. Social media addiction is a serious problem that is not given the attention it deserves. Children are becoming addicted to their phones and online worlds, and it is causing mental and physical damage. Like any addiction, it is difficult to cure once it has taken root. Therefore, preventing your child from getting addicted to online habits is a much better approach than trying to get them to stop using their digital technology all the time.

Screentime Strategies

Now that you understand the importance of helping your child develop a healthy balance between online and offline time, we must consider how you will implement it. Don't be surprised if your suggestions are met with some resistance, especially among older teenagers who have had unrestricted access to their phones for some time. You will notice that all the strategies and tools in this book work better the younger your children are. However, that does not mean you cannot make these tools work with older children. It will just take a bit more time and patience. So, let's consider some strategies for implementing screen time and screen-free time in your home.

Introduce Screen-Free Time During Meals

One of the best ways to foster a healthy online-offline balance is to reduce the time you and your child spend online at meal times. Instead of having dinner in front of the television, try eating at the dinner table instead. This will set the president that meal time is not screen time. A few years ago I was amazed by how a family of four, including two teenagers, I was visiting in Germany would have their phones on silent and away from the dining table during mealtime. The quality of the conversations that emerged and the mood around the table were impressive.

Eating at the dinner table promotes better posture and healthier eating habits. Eating at a table also helps your child develop a healthier relationship with food. Since they are eating without watching television, they are more mindful of what they are eating. They are also more mindful of their brain's hunger and fullness cues.

Furthermore, introducing screen-free mealtime gives you the opportunity to connect with your child. Since you aren't distracted by whatever is playing on TV, you have more time to talk about their day. This also allows you to check up on them. You are likelier to notice if something about their behavior seems off. They also have the opportunity to discuss with you any problems they are having. Therefore, screen-free mealtime is not only a useful technique for introducing a healthy online-offline balance, but it can also strengthen your relationship with your child.

Set Time Limits for Online Time

This one might be met with some resistance, but you could set a time limit for how long your child is allowed to spend online. For example, you can set an hour limit for online gaming in the evenings, provided their homework and other responsibilities are met. This gives them some online time daily without allowing them 24/7 access to their phones. Setting time limits can help your child realize that online time is meant to be a treat and they don't need to be on their phones or playing games all the time. It gives them more time to focus on other things, even when those things are not homework or studying.

Consider the 24/6 Approach

The 24/6 approach is an idea presented by Tiffany Shlain (2019) in her book, *24/6: The Power of Unplugging One Day a Week*. This technique involves disconnecting from all digital technology for 24 hours, one day a week. We'll share more about Tiffany's reason for this technique and how it has changed her relationship with technology in the following section. As you can imagine, having an entire day without technology can inspire your children to try something new. They can play outside, spend time with their friends and family, or pursue a hobby that is not online. This is a brilliant technique to combine with a fun family activity that creates a sense of balance in your child's life and helps them realize their lives don't revolve around their online connections.

Encourage Other Activities or Volunteer Work

Another way to instill a sense of balance is by encouraging your child to get involved with their community through volunteer work. Whether they volunteer at the outreach program at their school, get involved with the soup kitchen, or volunteer their time at the local animal shelter, encouraging your child to get involved in their community can help them find a balance between online and offline time. It also helps them pursue other interests and hobbies. As a bonus, they will learn to better appreciate all they have, and they will realize that access to digital technology is a privilege, not a right.

Teach Children About Gratitude

Tying in with the previous section, teaching your children about gratitude can help them realize how privileged they are to have the technology they have. Instead of rebelling when they are not allowed more screen time during the day, they will learn to be grateful for the time they are permitted to be online. There are various ways of teaching your child about gratitude. Being grateful goes beyond fostering a balance between online and offline time. It will help to nurture caring and compassionate children—something the world needs more of.

Allow Children to Find Balance on Their Own

As Jennifer Bernstein explains in *Smart Social*, constantly controlling online time is not a long-term solution for fostering balance between online and offline time (*Tips to Balance Time Spent Online & Offline*, 2017). While you can guide your child by introducing some of the techniques mentioned earlier, you must also allow them to find their own balance. When your child is younger, they might get bored easily and pursue other activities by themselves. Older children may realize how much time they waste online and focus on other things instead of spending all their time on their phones. Guiding them to find balance on their own will show that you trust their judgment and will make them feel more in control of their time.

Encourage Time Spent Outside

If your child is always inside playing games or scrolling through social media, the odds are they aren't spending enough time outside. Being outside has many advantages for your mental and physical health. So, when you introduce some screen free time in your home, use that time to go for a walk, visit the dog park, or have ice cream at the beach. This will help your children spend more time outside and help them see the value in time disconnected from the digital world.

Consider a Digital Detox Center

Many countries, including the United States, UK, and more, have established digital detox centers where people addicted to social media, or those simply wanting to detox from it, can come and experience the freedom that comes with a digital detox. These centers provide you with the support needed to break free from the hold social media has on your life. If your child is really struggling to let go of social media, perhaps one of these centers can help them do so. It might also be a good starting point for your family, as you will learn effective detoxing strategies at these centers.

Set a Better Example

As mentioned in the previous chapter, children copy the behavior we model. If you are constantly scrolling through social media, you are not in a position to tell your child to manage their time better. Instead, you must set a positive example. Volunteer at an organization that interests you, pursue other hobbies, and spend more time doing things that aren't connected to the digital world. This behavior will resonate with your children and they will follow it too, realizing that digital technology is not meant to be used all the time.

Choosing which of these strategies you want to use depends on your situation at home. I would recommend trying a few of them and seeing which ones work best. If your children are a bit older, you can also discuss these strategies with them and try finding the best option that works for everyone. Teaching your children to manage their online-offline time is not about dictating their every move, but about helping them find balance in their lives. Therefore, opening the floor for discussion and consideration will help them be more accepting of the new rules and techniques you decide to introduce.

If a strategy has been introduced during a family discussion, a follow-up meeting can be organized to assess how everyone feels about implementing the strategy. If an improvement is needed, work on it for the next meeting. In my family, we regularly have gatherings (ideally weekly) to evaluate our strengths and weaknesses and how we can grow stronger together despite the challenges we may face. While everyone's stories and needs are different, I believe follow-up meetings can help ensure everyone's needs are met.

Tales of Time Outs

Some readers may doubt the viability of the techniques discussed above. I would too, if I had not experienced great success with them. If your children are prone to being skeptical or outright dismissive of your suggestions and don't appreciate your interferance with their online time, you may question whether any of these techniques will actually help them. So, to help you discover the potential benefits of these techniques, I have gathered some success stories of families who have implemented these techniques with great success.

Tiffany Shlain's Success Story Using the 24/6 Lifestyle

Tiffany Shlain introduced a 24/6 lifestyle into her home when she noticed that she was getting more disconnected from her family due to being too connected to her phone. While it took some time for everyone to get onboard with the idea of going one day without technology, it ultimately brought her family closer together. Tiffany shares the following in her book (Shlain, 2019):

> A weekly day without screens improves our family's lives, too. Our daughters, Odessa (sixteen) and Blooma (ten), have done this practice most of their lives, and it's shaped how they interact with technology in extremely beneficial ways. They enjoy their time off screens and look forward to it. It feels like a vacation every week. (p. 106)

Sarah Lee's Digital Detox Story

Sarah Lee is a writer and editor who decided to take a digital detox for 24 hours after noticing that she was glued to her phone all the time. She explains in her article published in *Taste of Home* (Lee, 2017):

> I'm constantly checking my phone and working on the computer. I watch YouTube videos rather than read a book, and when I wash the dishes I listen to music through my phone. I noticed I depended on technology way too much and needed a break! (p. 7)

After detoxing from all digital devices for 24 hours, Sarah says that her productivity soared, she learned to appreciate the peace and quiet, she did more physical activity, and she felt calmer and was more connected to herself and others after the detox. If this is what a single digital detox did for Sarah, imagine what it can do for your children when implemented regularly.

Gemma Breen Changed Her Life in One Week

Gemma Breen (2021) never considered herself as someone who is constantly stuck to her phone. But she did feel like she was using her phone too much. So, when she was asked by her job to engage in a week-long digital detox with her family, she jumped at the opportunity. She, her husband, and their two sons committed to a week without technology, and Gemma noticed the following things during that week:

- Her children don't crave digital technology as much as she thought they did.

- She is not as busy as she thinks she is (her time online makes her feel a lot busier than she is).

- She was missing out on the sleep her body needs.

- Much of her stress was caused by the need to check everything.

- Her children were not getting the attention they deserved.

After noticing these things, Gemma and her husband committed to embracing offline days more often and continued seeing improvements in their family.

Ed Sheeran's Digital Detox Lesson

While you may think digital addictions are a "normal people problem," celebrities and influencers struggle just as much with this as we do. Ed Sheeran decided to do a digital detox in 2015, after saying he was sick of seeing the world through a screen and not with his own eyes. He used a break he had in his schedule to travel the world and take some much needed time away from his phone. While you might not be planning a world-tour anytime soon, encouraging a digital detox on your next family trip can help everyone enjoy the trip more and experience everything the holiday has to offer.

Tamara and Michael Reconnected When Disconnecting

Tamara and Michael traveled the world for six months in 2015. During a month-long yoga and meditation retreat in India, the couple decided to switch off their phones and all their other digital devices to get the most of the retreat. At first, it was difficult to adapt, but Tamara says as time went by she learned to focus on the present instead of thinking about what her friends and others were up to. Embracing a digital detox can help you and children focus on your time together and be present instead of constantly looking at the world through the eyes of others.

Key Takeaway From Chapter 5

In this chapter we considered the advantages of a digital detox, or time spent away from technology. We considered the mental and physical risks of online addiction. We also discussed the advantages of finding equilibrium between online and offline time, like helping your child see screen time as a reward for good behavior and helping them develop better social skills. We discussed various strategies for introducing offline-online time balance, such as the 24/6 lifestyle, time limits, offline mealtimes, and allowing children to find balance on their own. Then, we discussed several success stories that show just how beneficial a digital detox can be for your family and your children.

How social media use affects your child's mental health

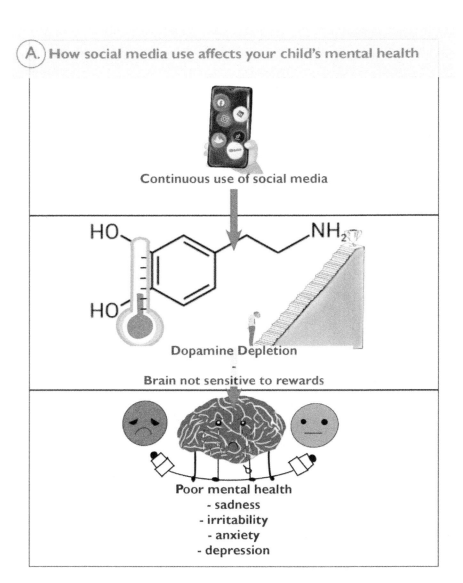

Temporary deprivation of social media

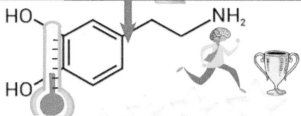

Dopamine Recalibration
-
Brain sensitive to rewards

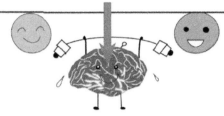

Improved mental health
- pleasure
- excitement
- happiness

Chapter 6:

Navigating the Tides of Cyberbullying, Sexting and Online Gaming

While we've made mention of the advantages of social media and digital technology in the previous chapters, we must also discuss its dangers. After all, the purpose of this book is to help you to protect your child against the dangers of digital technology. In this chapter, we will discuss three particularly troubling risks of digital technology—cyberbullying, sexting, and online gaming.

In a study published in OFCOM, the official UK communications regulator, parents expressed the following concerns regarding their children and social media use (*Children and Parents*, 2023):

> Parents expressed concerns about many aspects of children's media use, including being bullied online (70%) or via games (54%), but the most common concerns among parents related to their child seeing content that was inappropriate for their age (75%), or 'adult' or sexual content (73%). (p. 2)

Digital technology has many dangers and risks.. However, these three factors are what worry parents most. They can have detrimental effects on your children's mental health and may lead to various problems in all aspects of their lives.

In this chapter, we will consider the landscape of cyberbullying, sexting, and online gaming, the effects these factors can have on your child, and how to empower your children to counteract online harassment. We'll consider how you, as parent, can work with your school and community to keep children safe against these factors. We'll also share some success stories to help you see there is light at the end of this tunnel. Even if your child has fallen prey to these factors, they can overcome it.

Hidden Wounds: Exploring the Landscape of Cyberbullying and Sexting

Cyberbullying may be something you aren't too familiar with, as most of us grew up without this risk. While bullying has always been a factor in schools, cyberbullying poses a new threat. It can cause severe damage to your child's mental and emotional health and may even tarnish their reputation, or even lead to suicide. Sexting also has many potential effects on your child's life. Even if they don't want to admit it, many teenagers have experienced sexting and pornography, and it has a significant effect on their minds. So, let's consider what cyberbullying and sexting are and how they pose a danger to your child.

How Does Cyberbullying Work?

Cyberbullying is a form of bullying that takes place online. Nearly 50% of American teenagers report that they have experienced or been a part of some type of cyberbullying (Vogels, 2022). There are six different types of commonly recognized forms of cyberbullying. According to one article published in Pew Research Center, older teenage girls (15-17) are the most at risk for cyberbullying (Vogels, 2022). The six types of cyberbullying include the following:

- **Name calling:** Believe it or not, the same name calling that occurs at school is often also spread online. Children may become the victim of name calling and online harassment. Comments about their appearance and bodies are some of the most common reasons for name calling and online teasing.

- **Being sent explicit images they have not asked for:** Pornographic images are often sent to teenagers without them having asked for it. This is known as cyberflashing and often occurs without the child having requested or even wanting to see these images.

- **Spreading false rumors:** Spreading false rumors about someone is just as prevalent online as in person. Many teenagers have experienced false rumors being spread around about them, and some have also admitted to being a part of the online rumor mill.

- **Constantly being asked about whereabouts:** Some children experience harassment in another form. People other than their parents may constantly ask them where they are, what they are doing, and who they are with. This can make the child feel unsafe no matter where they go.

- **Physical threats:** Some children also receive physical threats. These threats can be accompanied by false rumors, though that isn't always the case. People may threaten online to hurt a child or the people they love.

- **Having explicit images shared without consent:** Revenge porn, as it is known, is when explicit images of a child or teenager are sent to others without their consent. This is a common form of cyberbullying after a couple have broken up, when one party will spread explicit images of their ex.

As you can see, these types of cyberbullying pose a real threat to your child. Some of the types of bullying affect their mental health. They might be isolated if false rumors are spread about them. They might feel as if they need to lose weight or change their appearance if they are attacked online. They might become depressed or suffer from anxiety if they are receiving threats online or being called names. They might also suffer severe humiliation if explicit images of them are being spread around online, or if they constantly receive explicit images they have not asked for.

Physical threats and stalking can also lead to physical danger. Your child may be at risk of being abducted or physically assaulted if they receive these kinds of messages. The worst part of cyberbullying is that children are often too scared to come to their parents with the news. They might be ashamed that they will be judged by their parents for sending or receiving explicit images. They might also fear getting in trouble if they have engaged in risky behavior and are now being stalked or threatened, causing them to avoid telling their parents about the trouble they are in. This is why it is so important to foster honest, open communication with your child and assure them that no matter what happens, their safety and well-being is your priority.

What is Sexting?

Sexting is the act of engaging in explicit behavior online. This includes sending messages, photos, and videos of a sexual nature to someone over social media or the internet. You may know it better as phone sex. However, the difference between phone sex and sexting is that sexting involves sending the images and information via text. This means it is on the internet, where it can be copied and forwarded to anyone at any time. Many teenagers have engaged in sexting and have sent explicit photos of themselves to their partners or friends. While children may think sexting is safe because there is no risk of getting pregnant or contracting a sexually transmitted disease, that is not the case.

There are several dangers of sexting, which we will discuss in the following section. You may also wish to know why children engage in sexting in the first place. Well, there are a couple of reasons why this can happen.

Children Sext Because They Think It Makes Them Cool

As children get older, they start exploring riskier behavior. This is nothing new, and you probably did a few "risky" things when you were a teenager too. Some children think that if they engage in certain sexual practices, like sexting, their friends will think they are cool. If they want to be popular or trendsetters at school, they might choose to engage in sexting so they are seen as being daring.

They Feel Pressured to Do It by Their Partners

Some children feel pressured to please their girlfriends or boyfriends. They might engage in sexting as a way to please them without having to do anything physical. This is an especially common occurrence when a child is dating someone older than them, or if their partner has engaged in more sexual experiences than them.

They Experience Peer Pressure

In some cases, children might engage in sexting because they feel pressured to do so by their friends. If all of their friends are sexting and it is a common topic for discussion at school, they might feel like they must do it as well if they want to fit in. In this case, they might also engage in sexting with strangers online just to say that they have also experienced it.

They Think It Is Harmless

When asked why they would engage in such behavior, most children say that they do it because it is harmless. They don't physically engage in any sexual behavior, so there is no risk of getting hurt. They can also keep their virginity intact while engaging in sexting with someone.

They Are Hormonal

Let's face it, teenagers are hormonal. Many children experience a rush of hormones during puberty and they don't know how to deal with these thoughts and feelings in a healthy way. They might seek a physical release and choose to engage in sexting to get that release. They might also just be curious about sex and the opposite sex and engage in sexting to learn more about these topics that interest them.

One of the problems with sexting is that it opens the door to many other sexual behaviors, including pornography and sexual foreplay. The more comfortable children become with talking about sex, the more curious they will be to explore other avenues of sexual experiences.

The Dangers of Sexting

You may already have guessed some of the dangers of sexting, but there are a few that I think are worth discussing regardless. Sexting is an extremely concerning practice among children and it needs to be addressed with a certain grace. Grabbing your child's phone and going through it to see if they have been sexting is not the answer, as it will certainly cause embarrassment and distrust in your relationship. Therefore, we'll discuss how to help your child in this situation in the following section. First, however, let's consider the dangers of sexting and the effect it has on the youth.

It Could Be Saved and Forwarded

One of the dangers of the digital world is that nothing is private, ever. Anything your child sends online can be resent and used by others. It therefore increases the risk of your child's explicit messages being forwarded to other people. In some cases, their pictures may even be shared to pornography websites.

Unwanted People Can Access the Content

Hackers can easily access your child's phone, regardless of the inscription software on their phones. This means that anyone can access your child's messages and use those messages for their own gain. They can sell the pictures, distribute the messages, and use these messages to manipulate your child.

Sexting Could Have Legal Implications

Sexting can also have legal implications. For instance, in the UK, the age of consent for sexual intercourse is 16. However, it is illegal to make, distribute, possess, or show any explicit images of anyone under 18, even if the content was created with the consent of that young person. If your child is a minor, it is illegal for images or videos of them to be sent around. If they are not a minor but talking to a minor, they would be participating in the distribution of child pornography, which is a serious offense and could lead to imprisonment.

It Could Tarnish Their Reputation

Should news come out that your child is sexting, or their images and content be leaked to others, it could seriously damage their reputation. They could also get into trouble at school since most schools have strict rules and policies against such behavior. Since this content is online, it could follow them wherever they go, affecting them for the rest of their lives.

Sexting Can Lead To Predator Behavior

If your child is sexting with someone they met online, they could be talking to a predator. The person they are sexting with may use this content for their personal gain. Your child might even be at risk for abduction or sexual harassment should the predator entice them to meet up.

Sexting Can Be Used for Cyberbullying

As explained in the previous section, sexting messages can also be distributed by your child's partner or ex-partner as a form of revenge after the breakup. This content can therefore be used to bully your child. And since it is online, the bullying can continue and follow them wherever they go.

The Psychological Effects of Sexting

The dangers of sexting should be enough to convince you that this is a serious problem and should be addressed as soon as possible. Unfortunately, the dangers of sexting are not the only threat this behavior poses. It can also have a severe psychological effect on your child. One study published in *ResearchGate* found that there is a relationship between sexting and depression or depressive behaviors (Raine et al., 2020). This same study also found that sexting is linked to suicide attempts. Let's consider some of the psychological effects sexting may have on children and teenagers.

It Distorts Their View on Sex

Sexting often contains a lot of explicit language and descriptions. While sexting, people often describe situations that are highly unlikely in real life. This means that sexting may alter your child's views on sex. They could either become scared of it because of a violent description while sexting, or they can become interested in experimenting with sex, leading to engaging in sexual activities too young. This was true for Billie Eilish and many others with similar experiences.

It Can Lead To Rejection

If your child starts sexting with someone and that person does not take the messages kindly, or comments on the photos or videos they send, your child may feel rejected. They can also develop an unhealthy body image and lowered self-esteem. If the person your child is sexting with rejects or teases them, they might also develop a distorted image of sex and their bodies.

It May Contribute to Mental Health Conditions

Sexting can increase the risk of anxiety or depression. Anxiety levels can increase if your child is afraid of being caught out while sexting. A negative connection with sex can also lead to depression and self-isolation. Furthermore, if your child is bullied after sexting, they are at greater risk for depression and even self-harm.

It Can Affect Future Relationships

Since sexting can distort your child's view on sex, it can also affect their future relationships. If they have a certain idea of what sex is or what their partner might want based on their experience with sexting, they might allow unhealthy things to happen in their relationships if they think these things are normal. Furthermore, sexting can lead to negative relationships or negative expectations of sex in a relationship when your child is older.

Nothing good can come from sexting. It can potentially disrupt your child's entire life and may affect their views on relationships forever. Therefore, it is crucial to warn your child about the dangers of sexting and protect them from getting exposed to it as much as possible. In addition to cyberbullying and sexting, there is another factor we must consider; something that many children engage in and might also endanger their mental health—online gaming. Let's consider how online gaming may affect your child.

The Effects of Online Gaming on Youth Mental Health

It might be easy to understand the effects of social media content, cyberbullying, and sexting on your child's mental health. But there are also negative effects of online gaming and video games on your child's mental health. Like social media, online gaming can become an addiction. And like any addiction, online gaming can disrupt your child's entire life.

Anderson et al. (2008) in *Longitudinal effects of violent video games on aggression in Japan and the United States* concluded that:

> Playing violent video games is a significant risk factor for later physically aggressive behavior and this violent video game effect on youth generalizes across very different cultures. As a whole, the research strongly suggests reducing the exposure of youth to this risk factor. (p. 1)

Excessive online gaming has been linked to the following mental and emotional health problems.

Online Gaming and Depression

Unfortunately, excessive online gaming has been found to increase a child's risk of depression. This is partly because of the nature of some of the games children are playing. Many of these games are violent and have scenes with poor language and violence. This contributes to feeling depressed and negative. Furthermore, children who play excessive games usually have a vitamin D deficiency from not spending enough time outside. Vitamin D deficiencies have been linked with depression and depressing thoughts.

Online Gaming and Anxiety

Online gaming has also been linked to anxiety (Purwaningsih & Nurmala, 2021). Because online gaming provides children with an escape from the real world, they might become anxious whenever they need to interact with other people. Instead of dealing with the factors that are causing them to stress, your child may choose to ignore the factors and play games instead. But this will only lead to more stress and anxiety later. And since online gaming takes up so much of their time, children may fall behind with their school work, leading to more anxiety during exams and at certain times of the school year.

Online Gaming and Poor Emotional Regulation

Online gaming is often used as a way to ignore your emotions and avoid the situations that lead to emotional responses. This may cause your child to become emotionally blunt. It might also lead to emotional outbursts when they are confronted with an emotional situation. They might become prone to mood swings and show increased signs of aggression, depression, and anxiety. Your child might also not be able to regulate their own emotions as well or detect the emotional state of others.

Online Gaming and Sleep Deprivation

Excessive online gaming may also interfere with your child's sleep, leading to sleep deprivation. This can increase the effects of mental health conditions on your child and may contribute to mood swings, depression, anxiety, poor performance in school, and physical health problems. If your child is addicted to online gaming, they might not want to go to bed at night, thereby interrupting their sleep and leading to sleep deprivation.

Online Gaming and Interpersonal Conflicts

One study found that people engaging in excessive online gaming had significantly more conflicts with the people around them (Adair, 2021). This is because of the nature of many of the online games these people play. Furthermore, the more your child plays online games, the less he communicates and connects with people in real life. This can lead to more conflict and fewer connections with people in the real world. The same study also found that online gaming communities are often toxic, leading to negative thoughts and emotions building up in your child and further affecting their interpersonal relationships.

Considering the severity of the effects of online gaming on your child's mental health, you may wonder how you can manage the situation. Fortunately, many of the tips discussed previously, including the tips for digital detoxing, and the tips we will share below, can also be applied when managing the online gaming habits of your child. It's important that you establish solid boundaries from the very first day regarding your child's online gaming habits and address any issues you see in their behavior as soon as it arises to prevent their gaming habits from becoming an online gaming addiction. Let's consider some more tips for empowering your child to counteract online harassment, even from online gaming.

Stand Out, Speak Out: Empowering Youth to Counteract Online Harassment

While you can do your best to protect your child against the dangers of the digital world, you can only do so much. A big part of protecting them is empowering them to take care of themselves. They should understand the difference between right and wrong. They should know what signs of danger to look out for and avoid ending up in those kinds of situations. So, how do you prepare your children to face the digital world and how can you empower them to counteract online harassment? Here are some tips to help you accomplish that. These are tips you can share with them to help them help themselves. As a parent, you can only do so much—the rest is in your child's hands.

Consider How the Content Makes You Feel

One of the best ways to prevent mental health conditions from arising from digital use is considering how the content your child is looking at makes them feel. If they feel light and happy while online, the odds are that they are viewing positive content. But if they feel sad, lonely, or threatened, they are likely viewing negative content. Since social media's purpose is for entertainment, they should focus on positive, uplifting content.

Train Yourself to Be More Careful Online

We've discussed this before. If your child wants to stay away from cyberbullies and predators, they should train themselves to be more careful online. That means not sharing private information with strangers, not sharing explicit content with anyone online, and not agreeing to meet someone they know online alone in real life.

Practice Self-Care Online

If the content your child is watching online makes them feel sad or threatened, they should have the self-discipline to stop engaging with that content. If their social media feed doesn't make them feel positive or energized, it is not worth watching. Helping them understand the importance of self-care in all aspects can prevent negative situations online.

Keep Records of Cyberbullying

If your child is ever in a situation where they experience or witness cyberbullying, they should keep records of the event. Taking screenshots and saving messages can help them make a case should the problem persist or worsen. Having the evidence to back their claims up will be hugely beneficial.

Don't Click on External Links

As children scroll through social media, they might come across many links. Some of these will be advertisements where they can buy products. Other links, however, can lead to scams and shady websites. They can also give hackers the access to use their device however they want or steal personal information. Therefore, they should never click on a link that looks too good to be true or directs them to foreign websites.

Don't Become an Accomplice

No matter how innocent your child is, it is so easy to become an accomplice with cyberbullying. If they share gossip they hear or comment negative thoughts on another person's story, they are part of the problem. Instead of participating in cyberbullying, they should consider how they can help the victim, or keep out of it entirely.

Don't Respond to Cyberbullies Online

When a child feels threatened or attacked, it's easy to respond with negative comments and try to defend themselves. However, this is not a solution to the problem. While your child should stand up for themselves if they feel threatened, they should do so in a way that doesn't come across as being aggressive. If they respond with aggression, the situation could be seen as an equal argument and not a case of cyberbullying. The best thing your child can do is keep records of the incident without responding to the comments.

Block the Bully

If your child is constantly being harassed by someone online, they should consider blocking that person from their social media platforms. If it is not a peer doing the bullying, and if they cannot convince the person to stop, the best thing to do is for the parent to block the access to their child's digital technology entirely. If the matter persists, you may have to involve the authorities, especially if the bully is threatening or exploiting your child.

Talk to an Adult

As always, it is strongly recommended that your child speak with an adult if they have any concerns regarding cyberbullies or online predators. No matter how they are involved in the problem, or what caused it, they should bring the problem to an adult's attention. In the case of online predators or hackers, they absolutely should inform an adult as these people can be dangerous to the child and other people.

If your child follows these tips, they will be more empowered to deal with online harassment and cyberbullying. While you cannot protect them from everything, especially not everything online, you can provide them with the necessary tools to protect themselves. Furthermore, just because you empowered them to stand up for themselves, it doesn't mean you are no longer capable of helping. By fostering open and comfortable communication, your child will likely come to you if they experience online harassment, in which case you can help them through it.

Working With Schools and the Community

Another way in which you can protect your child from cyberbullying and sexting is by getting involved in your child's school and the community. Doing so allows you to determine the situation at your child's school and in their community. If you can get involved with the school board, you can also help make a difference in your child's school regarding how they deal with cyberbullies and sexting. There are also several ways to make a difference in your community to help ensure your children, and the children in your community, are safe. Here are a few ways in which you can get involved in your community and schools to help protect your children.

Consider the School Policy on Cyberbullying

When getting involved with your child's school, it's important that you understand the school's policies regarding cyberbullying and how they react to these cases. If your child's school doesn't have a clear action plan for dealing with cyberbullying, it's high time they get one. If you are on the school board, you will have a say in how the school manages cyberbullying. Ideally there should be a clear plan of what happens when cyberbullying is detected, just like there is for in-person bullying occurring at the school. The school should have a code of conduct that includes its stance on cyberbullying.

The code of conduct should explain the repercussions for cyberbullying when it is detected. For example, what will happen to the children found guilty of cyberbullying and how will the school help the victims. It is crucial that your child's school has a plan of action to deal with this problem, as it is a real concern these days. The school should also have a clear policy and plan to step in when there are cases of sexting in the school, especially when this content is shared throughout the school and may harm the students.

Inform the Students on What Cyberbullying Is and How It Works

Your child's school and community should work towards informing the children of cyberbullying. Helping them recognize what cyberbullying is, how it works, and how it can affect them can help them realize how dangerous cyberbullying is and how much it can affect them. If cyberbullying is not taught as part of the school curriculum (which I feel it should be), then the school should consider holding a cyberbullying awareness seminar at school. While children might not like attending these seminars, they are necessary in some cases, especially if there have been instances of cyberbullying at the child's school.

This is another reason why it is beneficial to be involved with your child's school. You can raise your concerns if these matters are not addressed and propose solutions for these problems if need be. The more involved parents are in their children's schools, the more they are aware of what is going on at school and how the schools are handling situations like cyberbullying and sexting.

Teach Children How to Document Their Online Activity

Another thing your child's school can do to combat cyberbullying is to teach the students how to document their online activity. Doing so allows the students to gather relevant information if they are being bullied. It also prevents students from making false claims against each other. If they don't have any proof of their claims, the school won't be able to act against the students accused of bullying each other. Teaching students how to document their online activity is also a useful way of showing them how to be responsible online.

Create a Safe Space to Report Cyberbullying

When there are cases of cyberbullying in your children's school, they should have a safe way of reporting it. This requires some sensitivity, as students may be embarrassed to share the proof they have. Therefore, it is recommended to have female staff who deal with cases of cyberbullying involving girls, and male staff involved in cases with boys. Furthermore, it's also important that the school has a system of letting parents know when there has been a case of cyberbullying at school.

The school doesn't have to share details about the parties involved (except to the parents of those children, of course). But informing the parents that there has been a case of cyberbullying gives the parents the opportunity to have a conversation about the problem with their children and help them manage the situation at home.

Create an Anti-Cyberbullying Initiative in Your Community

In addition to addressing the cyberbully situation at school, you can also get involved with your community to help your child and the children in your neighborhood. Having cyberbully awareness talks at your community center or library, and discussing the topic in general can help parents and children become more aware of this problem. It can also help to spread the news faster if there is a case of cyberbullying in the neighborhood. Furthermore, it will help parents keep a closer eye on their children and watch out for any signs that their children might be involved with or targeted by cyberbullies.

Create a Space to Report Cyberbullying and Predator Behavior

If your community already has a program for cyberbully awareness, you can create a report system where parents and children can report cases of cyberbullying and predator behavior. A community WhatsApp group, Facebook group, or newsletter can help spread the word if there has been a case of cyberbullying. Furthermore, if someone notices suspicious behavior, like a strange person hanging around a park or particular house, they can share the news, alerting other parents and children to be more vigilant. As they say, it takes a village to raise a child, so we must work together in our neighborhoods to protect our children. Some communities have great apps and programs for these purposes, so see if yours has one and get involved.

Work With Local Law Enforcement

Another useful way to protect your children from cyberbullies and online predators in their school and the community is by working with local law enforcement. Law enforcement typically has records of predators and cyberbullying cases. If one of these cases involves your child or a child in your neighborhood, working with local law enforcement to spread the word and help catch the culprit is a great way to become more involved in your community and protect the children and families who live there. Sharing information about suspicious activity and suspected predator behavior in your community can also help local law enforcement keep an eye on things and protect the community.

Spread the Word

If your child has been the victim of a cyberbully attack or has been approached by someone to engage in sexting, it is useful to spread the word to other members in the community, so they can ensure their children are safe and stay out of trouble. You don't have to divulge private information about your child. However, explaining that a situation occurred and that the other parents should be on the lookout can help keep everyone safe. Reporting cyberbullying to the school can also help the school be proactive and prevent these instances from occurring in the future and help children deal with them more effectively.

From Victims to Victories

In the previous chapters we shared some real-life stories of ordinary children who have dealt with cyberbullying and the effects of social media and digital technology on their mental health. However, in this chapter, I would like to share some celebrity examples. These celebrities have also been targeted by cyberbullies. Some of them were children, and others were adults. Regardless, seeing how they overcame these cyberbullying attacks and did not allow it to get them down might help you realize that your child doesn't have to stop living their life and chasing their dreams because of cyberbullies. Just like these celebrities, your child can overcome this problem. They will come out stronger on the other side and will exceed your expectations if given the right guidance.

Taylor Swift

While Taylor Swift often makes the news headlines for controversial statements and record-breaking singles, she has had her fair share of cyberbullying experiences over the years. Taylor moved from Wyoming to Nashville during high school to pursue a career in music. Her dreams were huge, and she received a lot of negative comments from her friends and peers, who often took to social media to share their thoughts. Taylor still experiences regular cyberbullying and trolling to this day on social media and other online platforms.

However, she has never allowed other people's comments to bring her down. Instead, she turned to her family who gave her all the love and support she needed to chase her dreams in the music industry. They supported her through all the online hate and enabled her to reach her goals. Judging by the success she has achieved, it's safe to say that she overcame her experience with cyberbullying.

Tom Daley

Tom Daley is a synchronized swimmer who represented the United Kingdom during the 2012 Olympics. After failing to obtain a medal for his performance, Tom received severe backlash from people on Twitter and other social media platforms. They mocked his performance, sexuality, and even his recently deceased father. Tom did not stand for this, however. He took matters into his own hands, seeking legal counsel for some of the threats made online. He also did not let these trolls deter him from furthering his career.

When charities and anti-cyberbullying organizations became aware of the situation, they also reached out to Daley and offered their support. While Tom's emotional state and confidence took a hit after the cyberbullying attacks, he did not let these attacks stop him from chasing his dreams and reaching success.

Selena Gomez

Selena Gomez has had a long career in the acting business, starring in *Barney* as a child and having a lead role in *The Wizards of Waverly Place* which aired on Disney Channel. Given how young Selena was when she first started acting, she has also had her fair share of cyberbullying attacks. She received a lot of bad publicity after she and her former boyfriend, Justin Bieber broke up. She was also the topic of criticism for many after gaining some weight. To make things worse, Selena suffers from a condition called Lupus.

She has not, however, allowed the trolls and cyberbullies to get the better of her. With the support of her family and loving fans, Selena managed to overcome these online attacks and continues to have a successful acting and singing career.

Adele

Adele has been a musical sensation for quite some time now. Her voice is absolutely stunning and she has released several songs which nearly everyone in the world knows and loves. But Adele has also been a victim of cyberbullying for many years, particularly regarding her weight. The online attacks increased after she gained more weight after the birth of her son in 2015. However, instead of allowing the cyberbullies and trolls to dictate her success, Adele continued focusing on her family and music career, not even bothering to address the haters.

Adele may have lost some weight since 2015 and is now much healthier, but her weight loss has nothing to do with cyberbullying. Instead, it has to do with her health and well-being. Not that we mind that those haters are now deadly silent and may have learned not to be so judgmental of others. As the saying goes, revenge is a dish best served cold.

Leslie Jones

Leslie Jones became a popular name in 2016, after starring in the all-female reboot of Ghostbusters. While she did a great job playing Patty in the film, she received a lot of backlash and horrible criticism from online trolls and cyberbullies. Leslie was bullied for her race, appearance, acting performance, and even her deceased brother. Things got so bad that Leslie decided to do a social media detox for the sake of her mental health. That, combined with the support of her loved ones and fans, helped her overcome cyberbullying.

While the experience undoubtedly upset Leslie, she did not allow it to keep her down. Instead, she continued with her career in acting and has since starred in several films and shows.

These examples show you that even the rich and famous are not immune to cyberbullying. They also experience it, and just like your child, they will be affected by it. But with the help of their loved ones, they have been able to overcome this experience and made great successes of themselves. If your child is struggling with the effects of cyberbullying, perhaps you can share one of these stories with them to help them see that they can, and will, overcome it.

Key Takeaway From Chapter 6

This chapter focused on helping children identify the risks of cyberbullying, online gaming, and sexting. Cyberbullying is a huge problem for today's youth, and your child may become a victim of it at any time. Sexting is a growing concern and more children are engaging in this behavior. Teaching them about the dangers and repercussions of sexting can help them realize why it is such a serious problem. Getting involved in your child's school and community can help you, as a parent, keep your child and other children safe from cyberbullying and sexting.

It's important to empower the youth to become resilient to cyberbullying and instruct them on what to do should they encounter it.

Chapter 7:

Fostering Connection and Digital Citizenship

If you are on social media, and you are not learning, not laughing, nor being inspired, or not networking, then you are using it wrong. —Germany Kent

After the previous chapter, you may feel terrified of the dangers social media and digital technology pose to your children. However, it's not all bad. While there certainly are some dangers to look out for, there are also many good things your child can gain from social media and the digital world. Helping them understand how they can make a positive impact through social media by using their skills and utilizing digital technology in a positive way can help your child learn about their social responsibility.

In this chapter, we will consider how social media and digital technology can be used to improve your child's life. We'll also consider how they can use these platforms to improve the lives of others. Finally, we'll consider how children can use social media to be agents of change and make the world a better place.

From 'Likes' to Impacts

Social media may primarily be used for entertainment purposes, but there is a lot more you can use it for. You may have noticed that many companies have taken to advertising on social media. You will even see people advertising how to make money on on social media platforms.

But there is even more you can do with social media. You can make a real impact on the world and other people's lives with the various social media platforms, and so can your child.

If you guide your child down the correct path, they might be able to use social media to bring positive change to the world. Let's consider how your child might benefit from social media and how they might use social media to benefit the world.

Social Media Allows for Meaningful Connection

Social media gives children the opportunity to connect with others, regardless of where they are. Whether they wish to talk with family living abroad, connect with like-minded people online, or receive tutoring from global experts on a specific topic, social media makes this dream a reality. The world is a much smaller place with social media, and your child will not be constrained by their physical surroundings when using social media. Furthermore, social media allows children with physical disabilities to connect with others, even when they are not mobile enough to travel.

Social Media Creates a Space for Creative Expression

As mentioned before, social media creates a space for creative expression. If your child is artistic, they can share their work on social media, where like-minded people will value it, even if your child's classmates don't. And since there are all kinds of people on social media, your child is bound to find like-minded people who will understand and appreciate their content, even when you don't. Regardless of your child's interests, they will find fans and people worth admiring and following for their creative expressions online.

Social Media Provides a Space for Activism

Social media not only provides a place for talk. It also provides space for action. If your child feels particularly strong about something, whether that's an injustice in their school, a political opinion, or a social concern, they can share their concerns on social media and take a stand for what they believe is right. Since social media platforms reach global audiences, their causes will also reach much farther and they can gather more support as a result.

Social Media Enables Discussion and Awareness of Important Topics

Yet another exciting aspect of social media is that it allows for global conversations. If your child is interested in other cultures or countries, they can learn more about these cultures and countries by speaking directly with people from there. They will also gain more insight into the political and social situations in other countries, giving them a better sense of the world. They can also learn more about important topics, including social injustices and cultural differences from others, helping improve their cultural awareness.

Social Media Raises Social Awareness

Social media not only allows your child to connect with people from other countries. It also makes them more aware of the social situation in their own country. This can help them realize how fortunate they are and which social problems they are facing in their own country, or even in their own town or city. While you may wish to protect your child against these factors, it is important that they learn about the problems others are facing, especially as they get older.

Social Media Highlight Injustices

Social media can help your child realize the injustices in society. These include cultural injustices, racial and sexual biases, and injustices towards children, elderly, and the less fortunate. If your child understands these injustices, they can work towards solving these problems. They will gain a greater sense of gratitude for the privileges they have. Furthermore, they might become more aware of how they are currently being marginalized, helping them stand up against injustice in their own situation.

Social Media Provides a Platform for Charity and Support

Social media does more than make children aware of their environment and the global situation. It also helps them make an active change in the world. Children are able to get involved with fundraising activities and charity organizations where they can help others in need. They can also promote certain causes to increase support for the cause, thereby improving the awareness of a cause or person and helping them to spread the word.

Social Media Fosters Learning

Social media also encourages and fosters learning. Your child can learn so much about the world on social media. Of course, not everything on social media is true, but much of the information shared on the platforms may spark interest in your child and lead to further investigation and research. Certain social media accounts can even teach your child about health and well-being, safety, fitness, and science. The content on social media is literally endless, and may help your child improve their knowledge and skills.

Social Media Encourages Questions

Social media encourages children to ask questions about themselves and the world they live in. They might learn something new which could lead them to question if there is a better way to approach a current problem in the world. Social media helps forge and develop the minds of our youth. And while there are some risks to the content children are exposed to, any content gives them a better idea of the world they are growing up in and the one they will inherit. They might question the justness of this world and consider how they can make a positive change.

Social media can help forge responsible, socially aware children who are willing to do what is necessary to improve the world for future generations and leave it a better place than they found it. Therefore, social media can help raise a better, more responsible generation and give children a better idea of what they will face when they grow up.

Online Uprightness

An important part of learning to manage the digital world safely is learning how to be a responsible digital citizen. Teaching your children right from wrong is part of your job as a parent, and it extends into the digital world. Since your child will come into contact with so much different content and so many people, it's important that they know how to interact with these people. Teaching your children how to communicate online is about more than just keeping them safe. It's also about ensuring they use the right etiquette when communicating online and preventing them from becoming cyberbullies and reacting unfavorably online. So, how do you teach your child to be a responsible and caring digital citizen?

Treat People Online Like You Would in Real Life

One important thing children should keep in mind when they are using the internet, is that they are still communicating with real people. Reminding them of this can help them keep in mind that they are still talking with real people. If children are reminded of this fact, they will have more empathy when communicating with others online. It's easy to forget that another person sits behind every post, making it easy to feel like you can say whatever you want to them. However, it's important that your child remember they are talking with another person and that they be courteous and caring towards others.

Right and Wrong Exist on the Internet

Another factor that makes a good citizen is the ability to recognize right from wrong. This is true in the digital world, just like it is in the real world. Explaining to your child that just because something occurs online, it doesn't mean the action is any less dangerous or wrong. Explaining this to them may help prevent situations, such as sexting, watching pornography, or using foul language. Children must understand that what they do online reflects who they are in the real world. Simply being online does not make it okay to practice bad behavior.

Your Words and Actions on the Internet Are Forever

Not only is how you treat people online important, but it's also crucial to remember that what you say and do online are permanent. Bad mouthing someone or making fun of them, sending around inappropriate content or trying to force someone to engage in something they don't want to is just as bad when doing it online as it is offline. And, while you can deny something you did in the real world, what you say and do online are permanently tied to your account and identity. Therefore, your child needs to keep this in mind when deciding what they want to post or how they want to respond to other people's posts.

There Are Consequences to Your Actions

A child needs to understand that there are consequences to their actions. Just like drunk driving can get you in serious trouble and may hurt another person, so too can the comments you leave on social media. Bullying their friends, peers, or strangers online may have dreadful consequences for the other person. It might contribute to their mental health conditions or may even lead to self-harm or suicide attempts. Furthermore, some activity, such as distributing pornographic content, is illegal and may have legal ramifications. Children should understand that they are not invincible online and they need to be considerate of the effects their online activities may have on others.

You Don't Know Everyone's Story

It's also crucial that your child understands they don't know everyone's story based on their social media content. While some people only post happy, motivational images, it does not mean those people are necessarily always happy. Therefore, your child should not assume they know someone's whole story when they communicate with them online. Also, if someone posts a negative story, your child may think they are being dramatic and simply need to get over it. However, your child doesn't know what that person has gone through. Instead of addressing them with harsh criticisms and more negativity, they should consider if there is any way they can make the person's life a little bit better. Showing empathy towards someone online may make an immeasurable difference in their real life.

Part of being a good citizen is making the world a better place. As Desmond Doss so aptly stated in *Hacksaw Ridge*, "With the world so set on tearing itself apart, it doesn't seem like such a bad thing to me to wanna put a little bit of it back together," (*Hacksaw Ridge (2016) - Quotes*, n.d.). Guide your child to become a responsible and caring digital citizen intent on making the world, and the lives of those on the internet, a better place. Even though your child's kindness may not always be returned, you will both sleep better if you know that you did the right thing.

Agents of Change

If your child thinks that social media is only there for entertainment, they should think again. Many people right around the world are using social media and digital technology to make a positive impact on the lives of others. In this section, we will take a look at a few of these examples to show you, and your child, how they can be an agent of change in this world. How they can use social media to make the world a better place.

Not all children have to become doctors, firefighters, or lawyers to bring positive change to the world. Some of these examples show that it takes just one small act of kindness to leave your mark on the world and in someone else's life. These examples also demonstrate the importance of adult leadership and support in creating agents of change.

College Student's Campaign

One professor saw the need for change in his community, and helped his students fulfill that need. Dr. Andrew Selepak is a professor at the University of California. He realized that his students had little idea of how they could use social media to make a positive impact on the world. So, as part of their semester assignment, Dr. Selepak had his students start a social media campaign to raise funds for a charity or non-profit organization in their area. While the students quickly realized online campaigning is not as easy as it seems, they also helped bring awareness to an organization and help raise funds to support it. While Dr. Selepak initiated the idea, it was his students who used social media for good.

Voiceover Teens Donate Meals

Cassie and Sabrina Glow, better known as The Glow Girls, are twin teenagers. They are professional voiceover artists and singers. During the Covid-19 pandemic, they saw how much people were struggling to survive, and they decided to help those people. Not only did they donate a portion of their earnings to provide meals to the hungry, but they also campaigned on their social media platforms, helping to raise funds for more than 20,000 meals in total. Cassie and Sarbina used their social media following to help others and improve the world by feeding the hungry.

Podcasts to Help Teenagers in Need

When Gael Aitor was nine years old, he listened to a podcast created for couples struggling to cope after divorce. This got him thinking that he wished there was something like this for teenagers battling mental health conditions and other issues. So, he and five others started a podcast called *The Teenage Therapy Podcast*, where they share stories of teenagers who struggle with, and overcome mental health conditions. They also share expert advice, tips, and other useful information for dealing with these conditions. Gael told *Smart Social* that he started this podcast because he wanted teenagers to know that they are not alone and that other people feel the same way they do (*11 Examples of Teens Using Social Media for Good*, 2022).

Helping the Children of Fallen Heroes

Megan was 14-years old when she discovered just how many parents in the police force risk their lives every day at work. Being the daughter of a police officer, this thought hit home, and Megan decided that she wanted to try and help children and families recover after the fall of a police officer. Megan takes the fallen officer's police uniform and creates teddy bears for the family. By doing so, the uniform gets put to good use and the family has something that reminds them of their lost one. Megan relies on donations and funds raised from her social campaigning to buy the materials so she can create these bears at no cost to the mourning family.

Helping Those With Disabilities

Alex Knoll created the Ability App, an app that shares information about restaurants and amenities in your area that cater to people with disabilities. Alex created this app after seeing a man in a wheelchair struggling to open a door to a restaurant. This led him to research whether there were any resources that could help people with disabilities determine which amenities would cater to their needs. Finding none, Alex decided to create one. The app is free to use and is constantly updated with more places people with disabilities and other challenges can visit.

These examples serve as a reminder that not everyone is as fortunate as you or your child. Some people have difficulties you are not aware of, and a simple kind word or bit of support on social media can make a difference. These examples also show you just how easy it is to use digital technology for good. Even if your child doesn't create an app or start a podcast, they can still change the world for the better by being kind and spreading awareness of charity causes they believe in.

Key Takeaway From Chapter 7

It's easy to obsess over all the dangerous and negative aspects of social media. However, it's also important to recognize how social media can be used for good. Your child can be a part of that change and use social media for good by being a responsible digital citizen. Social media allows for many positive experiences, such as meaningful connections, creative expression, activism, and social awareness. If your child is a responsible digital citizen, they will treat others with kindness and empathy. They will realize that the rules that apply in the real world also apply online, and that their actions online have consequences. They can use social media for good or bad. They can also use social media to make the world a better place.

Chapter 8:

Nurturing Online Creativity and

Self-Expression

In addition to encouraging your child to become a digital citizen, your child should also understand how they can enjoy social media and how it can improve their mental health under the right circumstances. Until now, we've focussed a lot on the dangers of social media and how to use it correctly. Social media can also be used for entertainment and creative expression. If your child knows what is expected of them when using social media and which dangers to be aware of and avoid, they absolutely can use social media safely and enjoy it.

In this chapter, we'll discuss how social media can serve as a space for online creativity and self-expression, and how your child may benefit from using social media for these purposes.

Social Media: Platform for Creativity

I have said it before, but I'll say it again. It's easy to read this book and think that there are no positive aspects of social media. While it's important to discuss the dangers of social media and the risks it poses to your child's mental health, scaring your child into not using social media at all is not the answer. Instead, if you have established a close bond with your child by using the steps we shared in all the previous chapters, there is no reason why your child cannot enjoy social media. One way they can do this is by expressing their creative side.

There are plenty of examples of people who use social media to express their creativity. You can see this on nearly every social media platform, including Pinterest, Youtube, TikTok (BookTok), Instagram, Facebook, and more. People share their creations on social media, teaching others how to do the same, and use social media to connect with like-minded souls. Your child can do the same. Whether they are painters, writers, singers, comedians, or content creators, your child can use social media to showcase their works and connect with others who have similar interests. Here are a few additional benefits of using social media as a creative outlet.

Engage With Others

One of the greatest advantages of social media is that it allows your child to engage with others who share their interests. No matter where they are, your child can connect and communicate with like-minded people. This is a great advantage if your child feels isolated from others with the same interests. For example, if your child enjoys sketching but there aren't any art studios or classes in your area, they can find teachers, mentors, and peers online. Since many people post tutorials online, your child can also improve their skills and use social media as a free learning platform. In turn, they can share their works and showcase their talents online.

Experiment With Different Formats

Social media allows your child to experiment with different formats of creativity. They can post different styles of art online and learn from experts in different fields. They can also experiment with different art forms themselves. For example, if they enjoy writing poetry, they can make videos where they enact the poem, make a creative video with animated visual aids while doing a voiceover of the poem, or collaborate with another artist on social media to produce something unique using their poem and another artist's skills. Your child will gain exposure to different art forms, further increasing their creativity and allowing them to broaden their horizons.

Seek Feedback and Advice From Other Artists

By posting their creations on social media, your child will have the opportunity to learn from other artists. They can ask for advice and feedback from like-minded individuals. While there is a risk that your child's self-esteem will decrease if they receive negative feedback, that is also a part of nurturing the resilience they will need going forward. While your child's artistic education may be limited in your area, it is bottomless online. Your child can reach out to other artists and ask for feedback and advice before posting their work online if they want to, or they can view any criticism and comments they receive for their work as a way to improve. They should also remember that any comments, no matter how bad, affect the algorithm of the apps and lead to more views and advertising of their content.

Curate Your Portfolio

Your child gets the opportunity to curate their online portfolio. By sharing their work on social media, they will create an online portfolio that they can later use when applying to art school, jobs, or other events. Furthermore, the more they establish themselves as artists. The longer they continue posting their work, the higher their authority will grow. This leads to more people seeing their content and them gaining more followers. Eventually, they might also catch the attention of other artists or people who can provide them with new opportunities. Therefore, social media provides your child with many opportunities they may not have if they don't post their content online.

Follow Your Interests

Of course, social media also allows your child to follow their interests—no matter how bizarre. If your child enjoys a specific style of art, like Japanese cartoons (Manga), they can follow other artists on social media and learn more about this artform and how it works. They can follow their interests on social media, learning more about the skills they are interested in without spending more money or traveling a long way to learn about it in person. Furthermore, some artists and creators share different aspects of their creation process. Your child may get a more realistic experience by following these creators, as they share some of the challenges they have had to face on this journey.

Instead of Only Consuming, You Are Also Inspiring Others

Another aspect of using social media to express their creativity is that your child will be using these platforms for something productive instead of only consuming information. They will inspire others to follow their dreams and pursue their hobbies. They will bring joy to other people who enjoy watching their content. Therefore, your child can not only use social media as a means to express their creativity, but they can also use it to make a positive change in the world. Whether they believe it or not, other people may be interested in seeing what they have created and their content might just be the highlight of someone's day.

Social media provides a fantastic opportunity for your child to pursue their interests and grow their skills. If they use the platform for good, they will also gain good things from it. And while your child can express their creativity online, they can also learn from other like-minded people. Your child can join a community of supportive people who share their interests and inspire your child to produce even more content and follow their dreams.

Despite how much your child can learn and gain from social media regarding their creative expression, you, as a parent, can also help them accomplish their goals. It will take some effort on your part, but the rewards will be well worth the effort, especially if you enable your child to chase their dreams and become a success in their arts. Let's consider how parents can empower young voices and foster creativity among children.

Empowering Young Voices

Your child may wish to share information on social media and express their creativity. However, they might also be afraid of doing so. There are several things your child may be worried about when posting their content on social media. Fortunately, you can help them overcome this fear and uncertainty. You can help boost their confidence and make them feel more at peace when posting content online. But before we consider how you can help your child and empower the young voices on social media, let's first see why your child may feel insecure about expressing themselves.

Even if you think your child's insecurities or fears are irrational, you must understand how your child feels and treat them as though you understand their insecurities. Doing so will help your child feel like you understand them and that they are being heard. In turn, this will also help them open up to you more if they feel that you understand them. These are some of the most common insecurities children have when posting creative content on social media.

They Might Get Teased By Peers

One reason why many children are hesitant to post their content on social media is because they are afraid of getting teased by peers— especially if their content is not really inline with what their friends may be posting. While this certainly can happen, it's important to remind your child that even though their peers may not understand their work, there are a lot more people on the internet than merely their friends. This means that even if their peers don't understand their art (be it music, visual art, or dancing), they are catering to a much larger crowd, and there will be a lot of people who enjoy their content and appreciate it.

They Might Read Bad Comments

People are mean online. Not everyone is a responsible digital citizen. Some people might feel jealous of your child's talent or they might just not like their style of work and comment rude or even insulting things. If your child sees this, they might feel like posting their content was a bad idea. Their self-esteem might also take a knock after reading some of these comments. However, as I explained above, any press is good press. The more comments your child's posts generate, the more their content will be distributed. That's how social media algorithms work. So, even if your child's post has some negative comments, it does not mean that they won't still reach hundreds of people across the world.

They Might Compare Themselves With Others

Your child might feel hesitant to post content on social media if they compare themselves with other, more established, content creators. They might compare their work and feel that they are not good enough, or that their art isn't as good. However, even the most successful artists started somewhere. Your child's skills will improve and then they can look at their first posts and feel proud of the progress they have made. Furthermore, people in the same industry will not look at your child's work and criticize it. Instead, they will look at it for the potential it has and encourage your child to improve and develop their skills.

Their Mental Health May Suffer

Unfortunately, any of the above mentioned factors may negatively contribute to your child's mental health. They might start feeling more anxious or depressed. They might also react in an overly sensitive way to negative comments if they feel it is a direct attack on them. If your child is sensitive to criticism, posting their content on social media might not be the best idea for their mental health. However, dealing with other people on social media and combating negative comments is one way your child learns resilience and improves their people skills. Therefore, if you help your child to deal with these factors, they will be stronger, better people and rise above the negative comments.

Empowering Your Child's Creative Expression

Considering the possible negative effects of posting their content on social media, you may wonder how you, as parent, can help your child overcome the obstacles and express their creative style on social media without their mental health suffering for it. While you cannot prevent your child from seeing the negative comments or experiencing the teasing from their peers, you can support them in other ways and help them realize that they are not posting their content for the haters, but for themselves and others like them.

You can help them realize that they might become someone else's role model or they might improve another person's day. How can we, as parents, help our children express their creativity online and not let negative comments affect their confidence?

Be Your Child's Biggest Supporter

One of the best ways you can help your child boost their self-confidence is by being their biggest supporter. Even if you don't understand the art they produce or the content they post, you can still support their work and creativity. This includes liking their posts, sharing it with others, and always encouraging them to continue their work and content creation. You can also support them by learning more about the interest they are pursuing, as understanding it better can help you understand them and connect with them. Being your child's biggest supporter may boost their confidence and make them feel like they can do anything—even if they won't admit it.

Respect Their Boundaries and Privacy

While you may want to share your child's content with everyone you know, it's also important that you give your child their space. For example, if your child doesn't want you sharing all their content on your family groups or Facebook page, you should respect that. If you don't respect their boundaries, they won't trust you as much and it may lead to problems later. Don't force your child to show you their content if they are not done yet and never invade their privacy by going through their things when they are not home. This is not supportive and is not a good way to encourage your child to express their creativity.

Give Them Good Advice

When your child does come to you for advice, it's important that you give them good, sound advice. While you may want to encourage your child to chase all their dreams and reach their goals, sometimes, their chosen course of action might not be the best idea. For example, if your child is doing well with their art and making some money with the content they post, they might consider quitting school. However, this is where you, as parent, should step in and guide them on the right path. They can continue creating content, but they must still finish school. Even if they are doing well at the moment, they should consider their future and you must help them do what is best for the long term.

Be Honest but Caring

Have you ever seen an audition to American Idols or another talent competition and thought to yourself, "Couldn't that child's family have told her she is not good at singing?" While we want to encourage our children to follow their dreams, it's also important that we help them set realistic goals. Your child may be brilliant at one thing, but not so good at another. If the content they want to post is really not good, you should consider explaining it to them. Furthermore, if their content is inappropriate, you should also explain it to them. As a parent, it's your responsibility to guide your child and ensure they have a wholesome and positive experience when posting content online.

Following these tips can help you support your child's creative expression on social media. If all parents follow this thought pattern, your child will have a more nurturing experience online. In addition to following these tips, it's also important to keep communication open and honest to ensure everyone is getting what they need and is being protected and cared for. The online world can be a scary one, but it can also be a brilliant place for your child to express themselves and gain some independence.

Stories of Unleashed Potential

We've shared several success stories of children and teenagers throughout this book. But I'd like to share a few more stories one last time of teenagers who have made a success on social media. These teenagers have taken to the online world to share their passions, whether it's singing, visual arts, or interesting toys and artifacts they have sold online. Your child may use their creative abilities to start a side hustle as well, which is just one more advantage of giving them creative freedom online. Let's consider some teenage success stories from the online world. Feel free to search for these teenagers on social media to see more, and feel inspired, about the content they post.

Dasha Derkach

Dasha Derkach is one teenager who took her hobby of sewing to social media. When hair scrunchies made a comeback, Dasha applied her sewing and creative skills to start a business. Dasha makes beautiful scrunchies that often correlate with the seasons or holidays. Dasha advertised her business on social media, where she not only sold her products but also shared her designs. Even though Dasha used her artistic skills for profit, she inspired others to take an interest in sewing and creating products as well. Dasha is an example of just how easy it is to combine something you love with a business concept to create a side business that spreads your creative designs and generates some profits.

Andrea O

Andrea O is another example of a teenager who used her creative skills to start a business. Andrea's company is *Peachy BBs Slime* and she creates what can be known as designer slime. Her various slime designs contain fun colors and scents, interesting toppings, and creative themes. Andrea often posts videos of the slime and the slime-making process to promote her products. And while you may think that slime is intended for small children, Andrea said that she uses her slime to combat and ease symptoms of anxiety. Andrea often creates new and interesting slime designs, showcasing her creative skills while helping people cope with anxiety across the world.

Pierce Woodward

Owner of the shop *Brand Pierre*, Pierce Woodward put his love for upcycling to great use when he started making rings from old cutlery. At first, he posted his creations on social media, where he slowly gained a following. During the Covid-19 pandemic, however, Pierce's social media following increased exponentially. He also grabbed the attention of some wealthy influencers who showed an interest in his designs. They helped Pierce finance his own store, where he has been making and selling upcycled rings since. While Pierce has a physical and online store, he still shares his designs on TikTok where he has the biggest following.

Maddie Ziegler

You may know Maggie Ziegler from the TV show *Dance Moms*, but this dancer has gained most of her followers on social media. Maddie grabbed the attention of some influential artists during her time on the TV show, including Sia. She starred in several of Sia's music videos, which have more than six billion views on YouTube. Maddie continues to dance and has starred in several other shows and movies since starting her career. However, this young adult's biggest following still comes from social media, where she often posts snippets of her dance routines and inspires many other dancers and teenagers to share their performing arts as well.

Halsey

Halsey may be a popular household name these days, but her story started on social media as well. Halsey used to post videos of her singing on YouTube and Tumblr. She still continues to create interesting and artistic videos and posts on Instagram and various other social media platforms. While Halsey is now an adult with a soaring music career, her story started as a teenager with a dream on social media. Her career kicked off when she did a collaboration with *Chainsmokers,* a music group who noticed her social media content. Halsey is another example of how sharing your talents and creativity online can lead to breakthroughs in your industry and potentially launch your career.

Hopefully, these examples have shown you just how much your child can gain from posting their creative skills on social media. Even if their content doesn't grow into a business opportunity or jump start their career, they might draw inspiration from others with shared interests. They might even inspire others who are afraid of showcasing their talents online. Social media provides the perfect opportunity for your child to express their creativity and share their talents with the world.

Key Takeaway From Chapter 8

This chapter focused on how you can help your child express their creativity online. Social media provides the perfect platform for your child to share their creative talents, regardless of what those talents are. People have made a name for themselves making jewelry from old cutlery, singing, and dancing. There are no limits to what your child can accomplish if they share their creative skills online. While they might be hesitant to do so because they fear being judged or compared with other artists, you can help them overcome their fear by being supportive and honest. This helps your child appreciate the fun and creative side of social media instead of focusing only on the negative aspects thereof.

Chapter 9:

Parents—Write a New Digital Narrative

Now that we have neared the end of our journey to understanding the digital era and protecting your child against the potentially harming effects thereof while allowing them to use it for the good it provides, I would like to use this final chapter to review some of the core ideas we covered in this book. I imagine you might be feeling a little overwhelmed at this point, as we have covered so much in this book that is worth knowing and understanding.

I don't want you to feel overwhelmed. Even if you don't remember or implement all the steps in this book, even using some of them can help foster a better relationship with your child regarding their use of social media and empower them to gain all the benefits of using these platforms. So, to remind you of the most important parts of this book, and how you can help your child on their digital journey, I have dedicated this chapter to being a kind of refresher. Let's consider what we covered in this book and how you can easily help your child navigate the challenges and dangers of the online world.

Reflections on the Journey

The first thing we should recap is the most important steps along this journey. As a parent or guardian, it is our responsibility to protect our children from danger and allow them to grow up in a healthy environment. Children are sensitive to change, especially when they enter puberty. They become more sensitive to criticism and they are at greater risk for developing mental health conditions, including anxiety and depression.

These problems are often exacerbated by social media, as children as young as eight or nine start browsing on these platforms. Here, they are exposed to various factors that may damage their mental health, including body shaming, content depicting violence, cyberbullying, online abuse, sexting, pornography, and more. It is therefore our responsibility, as parents, to raise our children in a way that protects them from these elements. This includes protecting them against the dangers and risks of social media. As we have discussed, there are several ways of accomplishing this.

The Importance of Open Communication

One of the first techniques we discussed in this book is open communication with your child. Having a close bond with your child is crucial, as it encourages them to come to you if they have a problem. While openly communicating with your child may present some challenges, especially if you are not used to having this type of relationship with your child, it is a necessary step for building a strong connection and gaining their trust even when they use social media. Open communication is crucial as it makes your child feel more comfortable to come to you if they have a problem. Whether your child is in trouble because of something they did, or if their troubles are no fault of their own, it's crucial that they feel comfortable and confident enough to come to you if they need help.

Openly communicating with your child takes a lot of patience and time from you, the parent. You may not always feel comfortable hearing or sharing certain details with your child. You may also want to strangle them at times when they end up in trouble for doing something irresponsible or something you specifically told them never to do. However, if you want to continue building a strong, trusting relationship with your child, you must keep an open mind. There are times where you will act as a parent, and other times you will act as a friend or confidant. Establishing an open relationship with your child is easier if they are younger, but it can be accomplished at any age.

Setting and Respecting Boundaries

Just because you want to foster open communication with your child, it does not mean you should throw the rulebook out the door. On the contrary, children need stability and rules in their lives to help them grow into functioning adults. They also need a good sense of right and wrong, especially when using social media. Establishing some boundaries with your child regarding when and how they use social media can protect them against the dangers they might face on it. Boundaries like not giving out personal information online, not making any online purchases without consulting you, and not meeting an online friend without a parent present are good boundaries that will help keep your child safe.

Discussing the reasons for these boundaries is also important as it lets your child know that you have a reason for these rules and they are not merely to rob your child of their freedom. In addition, it is important that both of you respect the boundaries set forth. If your child has their own boundaries, such as how involved they want you to be on their social media platforms, you must also respect those. Doing so shows your child you trust them and makes it easier for them to be honest with you. If your child breaks the rules or oversteps the boundaries you have set forth regarding social media use, you must have a punishment system in place to show them that their actions have consequences. Remind your child that you are not doing these things to punish them, but rather to keep them safe.

Nurturing Digital Resilience

Once you have fostered open communication and discussed boundaries and rules regarding social media use, it's time you work on nurturing digital resilience. Your child will need some resilience when using social media, as they are bound to encounter some negativity online. Resilience will prevent these negative factors from overwhelming them and harming their mental health. Unlike resilience in the real world, however, you cannot simply leave your child to try it online and find out by themselves. This is because the risks online are too great to allow them to experiment with the dangers of social media before learning what they can and cannot do.

Instead, you should focus on allowing them to build their digital skills in a safe and positive way. This includes allowing them to experiment to some degree with age-appropriate content. They will learn how to gauge between safe and unsafe content quite easily. They will also learn how to stand up for themselves and their peers when using social media to prevent cyberbullying. And if you have a close connection with your child, they will know to come to you should a situation arise that they cannot manage themselves. You must learn to let go when teaching your child digital resilience as you will not always be there to protect and guide them.

The Uses of Digital Detox

If you notice that your family is drifting apart or your children are spending all their time on social media, it might be a great idea to introduce a digital detox. Yes, this idea might be met with some resistance at first, but it is something that could benefit your family significantly in the long run, as you have seen with the testimonies shared in Chapter 5. There are various ways to introduce a digital detox, such as implementing a 24/6 lifestyle, assigning certain times where digital devices are restricted, and teaching your children about gratitude. Of course, you have to set an example during a digital detox, so the detox will apply to you as well.

There are many advantages of a digital detox, including helping your brain see digital time as a reward. It also prevents addiction to social media and helps your child develop stronger social skills. Furthermore, you may develop a closer relationship with your child if you spend some time with each other without digital technology interfering with the bonding process. After all, social media is meant to be something you do for entertainment. It's not meant to take up all your time. A social media detox can help your child focus on other hobbies, spending time outside, and volunteering to give back to the community.

Building a Responsible Digital Citizen

Another important responsibility we have as parents is to ensure our children are responsible digital citizens. This means helping them realize that their actions online have consequences in real life. Teaching your children about right and wrong online and how to use social media responsibly helps foster respectful digital citizens. There are a couple of ways of doing this, including helping them realize that they are talking to real people when communicating online, that there are consequences for their online actions, and that certain actions have legal repercussions. Furthermore, setting a good example for your child can help them realize how they should behave online.

Building a responsible digital citizen helps your child become a part of the solution to ending the problems we are currently facing online. They could prevent and combat cyberbullying, end the sexting and pornography culture, and help the next generation see the positive effects of social media. Building responsible digital citizens may eliminate many of the problems currently contributing to youth mental health problems. It's important that your child understands how to act online and you can help them do so by setting ground rules and modeling positive online behavior.

Fostering Positive Online Engagement

Finally, as we discussed in the previous chapter, it's important that you foster positive online engagement for your child. You can do this by reminding them of the reason why many social media platforms were created in the first place—to share content. By encouraging your child to share their creative content online, they will appreciate social media for its intended purpose. Encouraging your child to express their creativity online can also help them inspire others and meet people who share their interests. Of course, there is also the chance that their passions will grow into a career, as is the case in some of the case studies discussed.

Your child might be hesitant to share their artwork online for fear of being mocked or critiqued. However, if they have adequate digital resilience, this won't be as big a problem. Furthermore, social media offers them the opportunity to express their creativity, build a portfolio, and learn from others with shared interests. In this case, the pros of social media outweigh the cons, and your child will be better off for showcasing their creativity. It's important that you are honest and supportive while respecting their boundaries when sharing their work with others.

Navigating the Unknown: Embracing the Role of Digital Mentors

As parents, we grew up in different times. Most of us did not have cell phones in our youth, and those who did likely had a monocolor which could only text, call, and play snakes. But things have changed dramatically and it's important that we change with the times to better support our children. When you read about all the dangers social media poses for your child's mental and physical health, you may think that the best option is simply to prohibit the use of social media altogether. However, as we have discussed in previous chapters, that is not a viable answer.

Not only will it lead to your child doing things behind your back, keeping secrets, and not coming to you if they are in trouble, it will also not prepare them for navigating the risks of social media when they grow up and are exposed to it. Therefore, it's better to allow the use of social media under the right circumstances and set a good example than to prohibit your child from using it and having no control or information as a result. The digital age is not inherently negative. In fact, there are several positive aspects of social media in this age as we have discussed in the previous chapters. Digital technology allows children to connect with like-minded people, share their experiences, express their creativity, and keep in touch with loved ones who are far away.

But just because there are many positive aspects of social media, it does not mean we should entirely neglect to inform and prepare our children for the dangers posed by these platforms. As parents, we must show adequate leadership and set a good example for our children to follow when using social media. This requires some effort on our parts, as we are not necessarily familiar with the various digital platforms our children are using. However, you will find any effort you put in to understand your child's world and the technology they are using will prove beneficial. So, how can we embrace the role of digital mentors for our children?

Learn the Basics

As discussed in Chapter 3, it's important that you learn the basics of the various social media platforms your child is using. Doing so will give you a better idea of what the platforms are used for. It also allows you to bond with your child as you will better understand what they are keeping busy with. There are various ways of learning the basics of social media platforms, including YouTube tutorials. You can also ask your child to help you with the basics if you get stuck. This can provide a bonding experience for the two of you. However, don't betray your child's trust by going on their social media platforms and trying to see what they are doing there.

Set Boundaries

Once you understand the basics of a social media platform, you can set a few boundaries regarding when and how your child uses it. Whether they want to admit it or not, all social media platforms pose some risk, and it's your job as their parent to keep them safe and protect them from these risks. While they might not agree with your boundaries, it's important that you enforce them and remind them of the consequences of not respecting them. You can explain why you have set these boundaries so that your child doesn't think you do these things simply to upset them. Having a few healthy boundaries in place can foster a healthier child and protect them against the dangers lurking on social media.

Communicate With Your Child

The difference between a mentor and a dictator is that a mentor is open to mutual learning and communication. Therefore, if you want to be a good digital mentor to your child, you must be willing to communicate with them. Communicating your needs and expectations of your child when they use social media can help them understand why you have proposed specific boundaries. Being open for discussion also makes your child feel heard and understood, helping avoid negative emotions and distrust. Communicating with your child also helps you understand their feelings and how they experience social media platforms. It can therefore help you detect if your child's mental health is deteriorating.

Set a Good Example

As mentioned previously, children copy our behavior. This makes it so important that you set a good example for your child when using social media. As the saying goes, "If it would embarrass you to share something with your grandma, you probably shouldn't post it." Don't engage in online disputes, become rude when speaking with people online, or become guilty of what could be seen as cyberbullying. Instead, teach your child how to be a good digital citizen by setting an example of the behavior you expect from them. This also applies when helping your child find balance between online and offline time. You cannot tell them to find a balance if you are always on your phone. Setting a good example is a brilliant way of fostering a balanced, healthy child. It also gives you more authority when explaining your expectations for your child regarding social media use.

Be Open Minded

Yet another important part of being a mentor is being open minded. While you may have some ideas about how a social media platform works and which risks it poses, you may also sometimes have the wrong idea. In this case, it's important to listen to your child when they make their case for why they should be allowed certain things online, or why they engage in certain online behavior. For example, if you feel that your child spends too much time playing online games, but your child explains that they are playing with their friends and really don't have anything better to do, you must be open minded enough to understand their point and adjust your boundaries and rules from there.

Find Balance

When trying to connect with your child about their online habits, you must find a balance between behaving like an authoritative parent and a friend, or someone they can openly communicate with. This might take some getting used to and will require a lot of patience from your side. However, if you always react like a parent when your child tells you something, they won't feel comfortable sharing things with you, especially not when they get in trouble. Therefore, finding a balance between being a parent and a friend is an important step for any adult wishing to bond with their child. It doesn't mean your rules don't still apply. Instead, it means your child can come to you with their problems without fearing that you will judge or punish them in the moment.

Learn From Your Child

You may be used to being the teacher. That's been your role for most of your child's life. However, when it comes to social media and digital technology, your roles shift somewhat. In this case, you may have to accept that you don't know everything and you must open the floor to learning from your child. This is also something that will take some getting used to. However, if you can wrap your head around it, you will foster a community of mutual learning in your home. Your child, especially if they are younger, may find it pleasing to teach you something and share a part of their world you may not be familiar with. Therefore, you must humble yourself and be open to learning from your child when the opportunity arises.

Empowering Tomorrow's Digital Natives

Now that you know everything you should know about helping your child survive and thrive in the digital world, it's time to take action. By following the tips shared in this guide, you will equip yourself for raising a responsible digital citizen. You have the power to empower your child to reach new heights; heights that the digital era provides. Your child has the world at their fingertips, and with your guidance, they can do anything they set their hearts on.

Helping them use social media responsibly and safely can also help them realize the benefits of these platforms and encourage them to use these platforms to their advantage. The road may not be easy, and you will find yourself in unfamiliar terrain at times, but you can do it. And when you do, you, and your child, will thank you for the effort you have put in to make this possible. Since the digital world is unfamiliar to many parents, and you may find yourself in a new role you don't feel entirely comfortable with, I would like to leave you with a few tips to inspire you on this journey. If you feel stuck, overwhelmed, or scared, remember these things, take a deep breath, and try again.

Tip #1: Don't Be Too Hard on Yourself

Many parents reading this book will want to implement the steps discussed immediately and get things correct from the start. However, that simply is not practical. There are so many factors that may interfere with your plans, including a child who has no interest in changing their online habits or sharing their digital world with you. This is new terrain for you, and it's important that you are not too hard on yourself.

Things might not go according to plan, but you have taken a brilliant first step by reading this book and equipping yourself with the necessary knowledge to help your child. You are doing well. Be proud of the progress you have made.

Tip #2: Reach Out if You Need Help

Sometimes, you may need some help. Nobody wants to admit that they need help with their children, and society may have you thinking that this means you are a bad parent. But reaching out for help does not make you a bad parent at all. In fact, admitting when you cannot do everything and getting your child the help they need is a sign that you are a great parent. So, if your child's online habits or addictions are more than you can manage, or if they have developed mental health conditions because of social media, there is nothing wrong with asking a therapist or professional to step in and help.

There is also nothing wrong with seeing a therapist yourself if this experience has been traumatic for you as a parent. You cannot take care of your child if you aren't taking care of yourself. Admitting when you need help is not a weakness but a sign of strength. Besides, if you want your child to turn to you for help you must be willing to show them that it is okay to ask for help.

Tip #3: Teamwork Makes the Dream Work

If you have a partner or spouse raising your child with you, it's important that you are on the same page regarding your child's online habits and teaching them how to be a responsible digital citizen. You and your spouse or partner need to enforce the same rules and show the same amount of interest in your child's online habits and posts if you want to succeed with the tips shared in this book. It's important that you present a united front when helping your child overcome the challenges they face online.

You must also both be willing to set a good example and commit to digital detoxes as necessary to help your child realize that you are not expecting anything from them you aren't willing to do yourself.

Tip #4: You Don't Have to Be Perfect

While it is important that you set a good example for your child, it's also important to realize that you don't have to be perfect when trying to change your child's digital habits and shape a responsible digital citizen. This is a learning curve for everyone involved and it will take some time to adjust your mindset and then get your child on board with these changes. You won't always do everything perfectly, and that's okay. As long as you embrace the journey and try your best, you are already doing well. Just like you don't expect your child to be perfect at everything they do, you shouldn't expect it of yourself.

Tip #5: You Are a Good Parent

I think many parents who have children with mental health conditions, or argue with their children about their social media habits feel like they are bad parents. But that's not the case at all. You have dedicated your time to reading this book. You have implemented the steps shared in this book. You have even made a point of learning more about the social media platforms your child is using. All of that is proof that you are a great parent. You are trying your best and you will succeed. If your child lashes out at you for implementing some changes at home, that's okay too. They are a child, and they are stubborn and want things the way they want them. But you are their parent, and you are doing your best for your child. That's the hallmark of a good parent.

Tip #6: Don't Give Up on Yourself

Just like you will never give up on your child, you should realize that you cannot give up on yourself. This journey will take a long time and you may feel at times that it will be easier to just give up and allow your child to do whatever they want on social media. But you know that is not the solution. You cannot teach your child to be resilient if you are not resilient yourself. Therefore, now is the time to believe in yourself, find your courage, and see this through to the end. You can do it. Don't give up on yourself or your child and believe that you can see this journey through.

Key Takeaway From Chapter 9

In this chapter, we reviewed some of the most important topics discussed in this book, including the importance of open communication, setting boundaries for your child, nurturing digital resilience, the uses of a digital detox, building responsible digital citizens, and fostering positive online engagement. We also discussed your role as a digital mentor and how you can be a good mentor for your child even when you aren't as versed in the digital world as they are. Finally, I shared some tips and inspirations to keep you going on this journey and help you see it through.

Conclusion:

Guiding the Way Forward

Congratulations! You have finished the book. Your journey to helping your child overcome the effects of social media on their mental health is officially underway. While this book may be finished, your journey is far from over. You have learned so much in the nine chapters of this book and come so far. Now, it is time you implement everything we have discussed in this book in your home. Seeing a change will take time, and you won't always be your child's favorite person on this journey, but you can rest assured that you are doing what is best for them and you are nurturing your child to become a better, more resilient person. Why are the changes we discussed in this book necessary? Well, according to *The U.S. Surgeon General's Advisory* (2023):

> Our children and adolescents don't have the luxury of waiting years until we know the full extent of social media's impact. Their childhoods and development are happening now... Now is the time to act swiftly and decisively to protect children and adolescents from risk of harm. (p. 13)

This means that it is up to us parents to get involved and protect our children against the dangers (known and unknown) of social media and digital technology. As parents and a community we can keep our children safe, but it requires a lot of hard work and dedication from your side. You must be willing to put your ego aside and learn. Learn from your child, YouTube tutorials, and this book. You must commit to a crash course on social media platforms, how they work, and their potential dangers. Then, you must construct a plan for how you will keep your child safe from these dangers by implementing certain rules and boundaries.

As you know from reading this book, though, social media is not all bad. If you teach your child how to use it safely and which dangers to look out for, your child can gain a lot from social media. They can use it as a platform to express their creativity. They can learn from other like-minded people who share interesting content on social media. And they can use social media to raise awareness for causes they believe in and make the world a better place. By fulfilling your role as a mentor, parent, and guide, you can raise a child who understands the risks of social media but who also understands what they stand to gain from it.

This book has equipped you with all the knowledge you will need to become that guide. Your role as a parent will change as you implement these rules and tips into your home. The role of a digital mentor and student will be another hat for you to don. But you will see great improvements not only in your child's mental health but also in your relationship with your child as you implement what you have learned through this book. By helping your child overcome the challenges and risks social media pose, you are raising a resilient, responsible digital citizen who understands how they can use the technology available to them for the betterment of themselves and others.

As a teacher and a parent I truly hope that you have found this book inspiring. Yes, we discussed some scary topics and you have a lot of work to do. But it is time we consider taking a more active role in the digital and social media lives of our children, just like we have in every other aspect of their lives. It's time we play a more active role in this aspect of their lives, and we can do so by following this guide and adjusting it to suit our needs and family situation.

If you found this book helpful or inspiring, please leave a review and tell me what you loved about this book, and what you want to see more of in upcoming books. I wish you all the best on this journey and hope that you will notice just as much change in your relationship with your child and their mental health as I, and the many other people reading this book, have when implementing these tips.

References

Adair, C. (2021, October 17). *Video games and mental health: How gaming affects your mental health.* Game Quitters. https://gamequitters.com/how-gaming-affects-your-mental-health/

Adeane, A. (2019, January 13). *Blue Whale: The truth behind an online "suicide challenge."* BBC News. https://www.bbc.com/news/blogs-trending-46505722

Anderson, C. A., Sakamoto, A., Gentile, D. A., Ihori, N., Shibuya, A., Yukawa, S., Naito, M., & Kobayashi, K. (2008). Longitudinal effects of violent video games on aggression in Japan and the United States. PEDIATRICS, 122(5), e1067–e1072. https://doi.org/10.1542/peds.2008-1425

Autuori-Dedic, J. (2022, February 7). *How to teach kids to be good digital citizens.* Parents. https://www.parents.com/kids/safety/internet/how-to-teach-kids-to-be-good-digital-citizens/

Ben-Joseph, E. P. (2018, April). *Teaching kids to be smart about social media (for parents)* - *KidsHealth.* Kidshealth.org. https://kidshealth.org/en/parents/social-media-smarts.html

Breen, G. (2021, June 23). I did a digital detox for just one week and it changed my life. Here's why. *ABC News.* https://www.abc.net.au/news/2021-06-24/screen-time-family-digital-detox-devices-family-children/100205766

Carlson, T. (2020, July 24). *Three ways social media encourages creativity*. Media Update. https://www.mediaupdate.co.za/social/149081/three-ways-social-media-encourages-creativity

Chavda, J. (2023, June 21). *3. Themes: The most harmful or menacing changes in digital life that are likely by 2035*. Pew Research Center: Internet, Science & Tech. https://www.pewresearch.org/internet/2023/06/21/themes-the-most-harmful-or-menacing-changes-in-digital-life-that-are-likely-by-2035

Children and parents: Media use and attitudes. (2023). In OFCOM. https://www.ofcom.org.uk/__data/assets/pdf_file/0027/255852/childrens-media-use-and-attitudes-report-2023.pdf

Data and statistics on children's mental health. (2023, March 8). Centers for Disease Control and Prevention. https://www.cdc.gov/childrensmentalhealth/data.html

11 Examples of teens using social media for good. (2022, March 10). Smart Social. https://smartsocial.com/post/teens-using-social-media-good-deeds

Emily Mizen. (2023). Social media and the impact on our teenagers' mental health - Parent workshop [YouTube]. In *Norfolk and Suffolk NHS Foundation Trust*. https://www.youtube.com/watch?v=dNeL5MRrJZc

Ginsburg, K., FitzGerald, S. (2011). *Letting go with love and confidence: Raising responsible, resilient, self-sufficient teens in the 21st century*. United States: Penguin Publishing Group.

Girlboss. (2017, October 20). *Her social media double life left her depressed & anxious—Here's what you can learn from her.* Girlboss. https://girlboss.com/blogs/read/how-to-keep-it-real-on-social-media

Gordon, S. (2022). *What are the effects of cyberbullying?* Verywell Family. https://www.verywellfamily.com/what-are-the-effects-of-cyberbullying-460558

Greyling, N. (2020, September 23). *What is the power of social media?* Digital School of Marketing. https://digitalschoolofmarketing.co.za/social-media-marketing-blog/what-is-the-power-of-social-media/

Hacksaw Ridge (2016) - Quotes. (n.d.). Www.imdb.com. Retrieved September 30, 2023, from https://www.imdb.com/title/tt2119532/quotes/

Hamilton-Smith, L. (2018, October 7). "You look fat in everything": Friends say teenage self loathing set them on path to depression. *ABC News.* https://www.abc.net.au/news/2018-10-08/friends-say-self-loathing-social-media-set-path-to-depression/10337414

Hashem, H. (2021, November 1). *13 Positive effects of social media on our society today.* Kubbco. https://www.kubbco.com/13-positive-effects-of-social-media-on-our-society-today/

Heathman, A. (2018, September 24). *Young people are using social media to push for change.* Evening Standard. https://www.standard.co.uk/tech/demos-facebook-young-people-social-media-a3942121.html

Hesse, B. (2015, June 29). *15 Times facebook and twitter improved the world.* Digital Trends. https://www.digitaltrends.com/social-media/best-examples-of-social-media-doing-good-deeds/

How do you use social media to spark your creativity and connect with other creative professionals? (n.d.). Www.linkedin.com. https://www.linkedin.com/advice/0/how-do-you-use-social-media-spark-your-creativity

How to teach kids to be good digital citizens. (2020, December 11). Kidas. https://getkidas.com/digital-responsibility-how-to-teach-kids-to-be-good-online-citizens/

Hughes, N. C. (2015, December 13). *Ed sheeran's social media detox lesson.* LinkedIn. https://www.linkedin.com/pulse/ed-sheerans-social-media-detox-lesson-neil-hughes/

Keeping myself e-safe - videos. (n.d.). Www.wmnet.org.uk. http://www.wmnet.org.uk/index.php?option=com_content&view=article&id=238:keeping-myself-e-safe&catid=13&Itemid=142

Kersting, T. (2020). Disconnected: How to protect your kids from the harmful effects of device dependency. In *Google Books.* Baker Books. https://www.google.co.uk/books/edition/Disconnected/9dXIDwAAQBAJ?hl=en&gbpv=1&dq=Disconnected

Kinger, P. (2022, March 8). Social media can empower kids to ace essential skills. *The Times of India.* https://timesofindia.indiatimes.com/readersblog/cornucopia-of-stirring-words/social-media-can-empower-kids-to-ace-essential-skills-41691/

Lee, A. Y., & Hancock, J. T. (2023). Developing digital resilience: An educational intervention improves elementary students' response to digital challenges. *Computers and Education Open*, 100144. https://doi.org/10.1016/j.caeo.2023.100144

Lee, S. (2017, July 3). *I tried a digital detox & here's what happened.* Taste of Home. https://www.tasteofhome.com/article/the-surprising-benefits-of-a-digital-detox/

Let's talk about sexting. (2019, March 25). Kids Helpline. https://kidshelpline.com.au/parents/issues/sexting-and-impacts-young-people

Locations - Digital Detox Log Cabins. (n.d.). Unplugged digital detox cabins. Retrieved October 1, 2023, from https://unplugged.rest/cabin-locations

Lua, A. (2023, March 15). *21 Top social media sites to consider for your brand in 2022.* Buffer Library. https://buffer.com/library/social-media-sites/

Mankato. (2020). The effect social media has on student mental health [Youtube]. In *Minnesota State University.* https://www.youtube.com/watch?v=-GkimR-FAm4

Mental health disorders in adolescents. (2017, July). ACOG. https://www.acog.org/clinical/clinical-guidance/committee-opinion/articles/2017/07/mental-health-disorders-in-adolescents

Mental health of adolescents. (2021, November 17). World Health Organization. https://www.who.int/news-room/fact-sheets/detail/adolescent-mental-health

Miller, C. (2022, October 11). *How anxiety affects teenagers.* Child Mind Institute. https://childmind.org/article/signs-of-anxiety-in-teenagers/

Mosley, B. (2023, May 11). *Social media and the impact on our teenagers' mental health - Parent workshop.* Norfolk and Suffolk NHS Foundation Trust; Youtube. https://www.youtube.com/watch?v=dNeL5MRrJZc

Noble, F. (2015, September 24). *Young couple who switched off their mobiles for a "digital detox."* Mail Online. https://www.dailymail.co.uk/news/article-3246874/How-young-couple-survived-digital-detox-switching-mobiles.html

Overcoming cyberbullying: 5 famous stories. (2020, November 19). FlashStart. https://flashstart.com/5-famous-role-models-who-overcame-cyberbullying/

Parnell, B. (2017). Is social media hurting your mental health? [Youtube]. In *TEDxRyersonU.* Tedx Talks. https://www.youtube.com/watch?v=Czg_9C7gw0o

Patel, M. (n.d.). The resilient woman: Overcoming adversity and striving in life. In *Amazon.* Amazon Books. https://www.amazon.com/Resilient-Woman-Overcoming-Adversity-Striving-ebook/dp/B0C7KTBHRP/ref=tmm_kin_swatch_0?_encoding=UTF8&qid=&sr=

Pin on the parenting adventures. (n.d.). Pinterest. Retrieved September 21, 2023, from https://za.pinterest.com/pin/309270699415334237/

Protect your child from pornography. (n.d.). Jehovah's Witnesses.org. https://www.jw.org/en/bible-teachings/family/protect-your-child-from-pornography/

Psyche. (2013, April 22). Good Therapy. https://www.goodtherapy.org/blog/psychpedia/psyche

Purwaningsih, E., & Nurmala, I. (2021). The impact of online game addiction on adolescent mental health: A systematic review and meta-analysis. *Open Access Macedonian Journal of Medical Sciences.* https://oamjms.eu/index.php/mjms/article/view/6234

Raine, G. A., Scott, R., Khouja, C., & Wright, K. (2020). Pornography use and sexting amongst children and young people: a systematic overview of reviews. https://www.researchgate.net/publication/346676980_Pornog raphy_use_and_sexting_amongst_children_and_young_people _a_systematic_overview_of_reviews

Rees, J. (2022, September 26). *How to balance life online and offline in 12 steps.* The Code of Style. https://thecodeofstyle.com/2022/09/26/how-to-balance-life-online-and-offline-in-12-steps/

Reuters. (2021, December 15). *Billie Eilish says watching porn as a child "destroyed my brain."* The Guardian. https://www.theguardian.com/music/2021/dec/15/billie-eilish-says-watching-porn-gave-her-nightmares-and-destroyed-my-brain

Richardson, J., & Samara, V. (2020). Easy steps to help your child become a digital citizen. In *Council of Europe Education for Democracy.* https://rm.coe.int/easy-steps-to-help-your-child-become-a-digital-citizen/16809e2d1d

Robinson, L., & Smith, M. (2020, September). *Social media and mental health.* HelpGuide. https://www.helpguide.org/articles/mental-health/social-media-and-mental-health.htm

Rutledge, P. B. (2022, August 23). *8 Ways to build a digitally resilient kid | Psychology Today.* Www.psychologytoday.com. https://www.psychologytoday.com/intl/blog/positively-media/202208/8-ways-build-digitally-resilient-kid

Shlain, T. (2019). 24/6: The power of unplugging one day a week. In *Amazon.* Gallery Books. https://www.amazon.com/24-Power-Unplugging-One-Week/dp/1982116862

Signs and symptoms of cell phone addiction. (2013). PsychGuides. https://www.psychguides.com/behavioral-disorders/cell-phone-addiction/signs-and-symptoms/

Social media. (2021, December 2). *NSPCC.* https://www.nspcc.org.uk/keeping-children-safe/online-safety/social-media/

Social media and youth mental health: The U.S. Surgeon General's advisory. (2023). Department of Health and Human Services. https://www.hhs.gov/sites/default/files/sg-youth-mental-health-social-media-advisory.pdf

Sun, H., Yuan, C., Qian, Q., He, S., & Luo, Q. (2022). Digital resilience among individuals in school education settings: A concept analysis based on a scoping review. *Frontiers in Psychiatry, 13.* https://doi.org/10.3389/fpsyt.2022.858515

Surgeon general issues warning on social media and youth mental health. (2023). [YouTube]. In *CBS New York.* https://www.youtube.com/watch?v=huktB4bfQtk

T, R. (2022, November 26). *Where to go for a digital detox in California.* California.com. https://www.california.com/where-to-go-for-a-digital-detox-in-california/

Teen depression - Symptoms and causes. (2022, August 12). Mayo Clinic. https://www.mayoclinic.org/diseases-conditions/teen-depression/symptoms-causes/syc-20350985

Teen depression—Why? What can help? (n.d.). JW.ORG. Retrieved September 11, 2023, from https://www.jw.org/en/library/magazines/awake-no1-2017-february/teen-depression-help/

Tips to balance time spent online & offline. (2017, April 16). SmartSocial. https://smartsocial.com/post/balance-time-spent-online

Twenge, J. M. (2017). *IGen: Why today's super-connected kids are growing up less rebellious, more tolerant, less happy--and completely unprepared for adulthood--and what that means for the rest of us.* In Google Books. Simon and Schuster. https://www.google.co.uk/books/edition/IGen/50MyDwAA QBAJ?hl=en&gbpv=1

van Dijk, J., & Poell, T. (2013, June). *Understanding social media logic.* ResearchGate. https://www.researchgate.net/publication/263566996_Unders tanding_Social_Media_Logic

27 Social media quotes with images. (n.d.). Readbeach Quotes. Retrieved September 28, 2023, from https://readbeach.com/quotes/tag/social-media

Vogels, E. (2022, December 15). *Teens and cyberbullying 2022.* Pew Research Center. https://www.pewresearch.org/internet/2022/12/15/teens-and-cyberbullying-2022/

Wang, Y., Dai, Y., Li, H., & Song, L. (2021, June 24). *Social media and attitude change: Information booming promote or resist persuasion?* Frontiers. https://www.frontiersin.org/articles/10.3389/fpsyg.2021.5960 71

What can schools do to help with cyberbullying? (2023, February 15). Delete Cyberbullying. https://www.endcyberbullying.net/blog/what-can-schools-do-to-help-with-cyberbullying

Why reject the media stereotype of girls? (n.d.). JW.ORG. https://www.jw.org/en/bible-teachings/teenagers/ask/media-stereotype-girls/

Wilson, J. (n.d.). *The dangers of sexting.* Centerstone Teen. https://centerstone.org/teen/media/sexting

Woda, S. (2018, December 20). *7 Consequences of teen sexting.* UKnowKids. https://resources.uknowkids.com/blog/bid/177105/7-consequences-of-teen-sexting

Young, A. (2023). *Pressures and dangers of social media: A personal story.* Www.leehealth.org. https://www.leehealth.org/health-and-wellness/healthy-news-blog/mental-health/pressures-and-dangers-of-social-media-a-personal-story

Printed in Great Britain
by Amazon

42443993R00098